BLURRING THE BOUNDARIES

Blurring the Boundaries

EXPLORATIONS to the FRINGES of NONFICTION

EDITED BY B.J. HOLLARS

UNIVERSITY OF NEBRASKA PRESS | LINCOLN AND LONDON

Acknowledgments for the use of
copyrighted material appear on
pages ix–x, which constitute an
extension of the copyright page.

Library of Congress
Cataloging-in-Publication Data
Blurring the boundaries:
explorations to the fringes of
nonfiction / edited by B.J. Hollars.
p. cm.
Includes bibliographical references.
ISBN 978-0-8032-3648-6 (pbk.:
alk. paper) 1. American prose
literature—21st century. 2.
Creative nonfiction. I. Hollars, B. J.
PS659.2.B58 2013
818'.609—dc23   2012029689

Set in Quadraat and Quadraat Sans
by Laura Wellington.
Designed by Nathan Putens.

Contents

Acknowledgments

This book would not have been possible without the support of a number of editors, agents, and permissions folks, including Kristen Rowley, Jodi Hammerwold, Matt McGowan, and Frederick T. Courtright.

Likewise, I am indebted to many presses as well, first and foremost the University of Nebraska Press for allowing me the opportunity to piece this project together, but also Graywolf Press, Counterpoint Press, and New Directions, all of which allowed me to further share their writers' works with the world.

Also, a thank you to my colleagues at both the University of Alabama and the University of Wisconsin–Eau Claire—your support has proved invaluable.

A special and heartfelt thank you to the writers showcased herein, all of whom worked diligently to blur the boundaries of genre by taking all the right risks.

And to the readers as well, may you carve out your own fresh terrain.

And finally, to my wife, who put up with my constant yammering about my own boundless enthusiasm for this work.

I hope you feel the same.

"The Eighteenth Week" was originally published in *Passages North* 31.1 (2010): 79–82.

"Time and Distance Overcome" was originally published in *Notes from No Man's Land: American Essays.* © 2009 by Eula Biss. "On 'Time and Distance Overcome': The Rewards of Research" © 2013 by Eula Biss.

"An Essay and a Story about Mötley Crüe" was originally published in *Opium* (2009). © 2009 by Ryan Boudinot. "On 'An Essay and a Story

BLURRING THE BOUNDARIES

B.J. Hollars

Introduction

Let the Blurring Begin

This is a story I've been told for most of my life.

In the spring of 1964 my grandfather drove his wife and three children to the top of the Alps until they could drive no farther. Without warning, the road suddenly narrowed, steepened; finding himself trapped in a particularly unforgiving slice of terrain, my grandfather was forced to make a choice.

"The choice" (as it is now affectionately known to my family) was whether the thirty-eight-year-old husband and father of three would get them out of the jam by easing the car's wheels forward along the edge of the mountainside or take the safer bet—reversing out from the direction he'd just come.

This is where the stories begin to diverge. According to my aunt—thirteen at the time, and the oldest of the children confined to the backseat—my grandfather pressed the automobile forward, though not before taking a few precautionary measures. The way she tells it, he handed over his wallet and insurance card to his wife, then waved her and the kids out of the car. The four watched as my grandfather's hands manned the wheel, creeping the white Corvair across the narrow roadway, bypassing the drop-off by inches.

My mother, the youngest of the children, remembers it far differently. While she, too, recalls her father handing over the wallet and insurance card prior to shooing them all away, in her version my grandfather does *not* drive forward but rather begins the slow business of turning the car *around*.

"He was attempting a ten-point turn," my mother remembers. "He'd drive it forward a few inches and then reverse it. And after enough of this, he eventually got the thing turned around and drove us back down to safety."

Yet most surprising of all is my uncle's version. He is the middle child chronologically and, quite appropriately, the one situated snugly between his sisters. When asked of his recollections from that day, he offered not only a different version, but a far different tone as well.

To his memory, *nobody ever left the car*. His mother remained on the passenger's side while the children in back peered over the edge of the cliff.

"But we were never in any real danger," my uncle joked, downplaying the crisis. "That is, as long as our parachutes opened."

For years, I have tried to write about this near-missed mountaintop disaster that occurred over half a century ago. Yet I've struggled to do justice to the story, mostly due to the many conflicting reports. To date, my most successful attempt was to write of it in the form of a Venn diagram, in which the outer regions of the circles recounted the varied versions of the tale while the intersection of the circles remained utterly blank.

While my Venn diagram approach, too, proved ultimately unsuccessful, its unique form seemed to explain why: a story as death defying as this demands a bit more overlap.

After all, how is it that my aunt, uncle, and mother could offer three wildly different interpretations of an event at which they were all present? While I expected a few minor discrepancies (perhaps a disagreement on the make and model of the car), quite surprisingly, the make and model of the car seemed to be the only details on which they could all agree.

My grandparents—whose adult impressions could have easily offered a ruling on the most accurate interpretation—passed away nearly two decades back, leading me to believe that the truth had died with them. However, in my most recent attempt at writing of this event, I stumbled on some new information that I believed might finally put the matter to rest.

My grandparents, both writers themselves, took turns documenting their European adventure in a humorous though unpublished book titled "Five Is an Odd Number." I came across several drafts of their collaboration a few weeks back, though surprisingly, not a single version directly addressed "the choice" on the mountainside.

Thankfully, their work did clear up at least one issue. While my aunt and mother have long disagreed even on what section of the Alps they were in (French or Swiss), my grandfather's written account sets the record straight; they weren't in the Alps at all, but the Jura Mountains of Switzerland.

"To the Swiss they are mere foothills in comparison with the Alps, but to Americans from the flatlands of Indiana, they are positively frightening," he wrote. "It would be here that our overloaded little Corvair would have its trial run."

Yet my grandfather's mention of the "trial run" was as specific as either of my grandparents ever got.

In a later section my grandfather adds that the Swiss roads were "excellent" though "rather narrow" and that the guardrails "although psychologically comforting, probably wouldn't prevent you from crashing down the mountainside should the worst happen." Even when the opportunity presented itself, my grandfather fails to mention that "the worst" nearly happened to him.

Pages later he offers one final clue: "The Corvair behaved admirably on the Jura Mountains; we were in low gear most of the way, but we made it."

They had made it, and according to my grandparents' account, the drive had proceeded without incident.

I chalked up this obvious omission as my grandparents' attempt at maintaining an otherwise humorous tone. By inserting such a dire scene, they would risk the form they'd established. They'd hoped to tell a whimsical tale of a family overseas (not a family over a mountainside) and by inserting the tale they might never have been able to return to their much-preferred lighthearted tone.

Having been born twenty years after that day on the mountainside, I am in no position to speculate on their "writerly" choices. Yet it seemed odd to me that the scene was omitted entirely, and this decision forced me to face a difficult question related to my own work:

How am I—so far removed from the tale—ever to tell it truthfully?

I am not the only nonfiction writer to face such a struggle. Nonfiction writers regularly grapple with this feeling-out process, pressing our hands to the past in an effort to report or reshape what we thought we always knew. Throughout this process we often find that we hardly know the half of it, and even the half we think we know regularly remains uncertain. Yet this uncertainty need not be a roadblock, but an opportunity—a chance to tell it new.

Collected here are the works of twenty writers, all of whom have endeavored to do just that—explore the new terrain of the nonfiction genre. They have all set out on their own perilous journeys, planting flags on far-off lands while plotting pathways into the future.

I should warn you: no two essays are the same here. While there are a number of serendipitous connections throughout (read closely, you'll find them), what remains most interesting is that while two essays may share a theme or a subject, the writers' unique stylistic approaches provide vastly different reading experiences. Despite the varied approaches exhibited in the work, each writer undertook the boundary-stretching challenge with a shared purpose—to take nonfiction to new and innovative places.

As noted, this "boundary stretching" is demonstrated in a variety of ways. While writers such as Marcia Aldrich, Kim Dana Kupperman, Michael Martone, and Ander Monson all experimented with the limitations of structure—offering an assortment of diagrams, fragments, formats, and outlines—others, including Monica Berlin, Steven Church, Susan Neville, and Ryan Van Meter, toyed with perspective and point of view. Others still—including Eula Biss and Ashley Butler—bridged the divide between yesterday, today, and tomorrow by resurrecting the ghosts of history, while Stuart Dybek and Ryan Boudinot experimented with the comic memoir, recounting a past that once was (or, in the case of Boudinot, never was entirely). Other writers stretched in terms of subject matter, explicating on the inexplicable nature of human nature, as demonstrated by Naomi Kimbell, Paul Maliszewski, and Brian Oliu—all of whom searched inward first before culling the stories back out. And there are many other boundary stretches, too, like Lia Purpura's epiphanic essay and Wendy Rawlings's and Beth Ann Fennelly's private obsessions that soon become our own. And finally, let's not forget Dinty W. Moore and Robin Hemley—two veteran writers who take another tack altogether: focusing on their first drafts and their works-in-progress to teach us what might be gleaned from our early attempts.

These experiments in craft offer a single and less than shocking conclusion: the boundaries of genre remain unique for each writer. Yet we also learn that writers uncover this new ground by their refusal to take the well-marked route. Much like a white Corvair on a mountainside half a century ago, we writers are all teetering on precipices of our own making, secretly seeking a safe way down but proud of our risks all the same.

A final word for what you can expect to find here: essays, of course, but essays that are meant not merely to be read but to be studied as well. As such, each essay is accompanied by a behind-the-scenes look at the writer's reflections on his or her piece, allowing the reader the opportunity to spend some time inside the author's head, studying the moves and the missteps that proved crucial for the final product. While I admit that essays are not frogs (and therefore struggle upon dissection), the authors' willingness to wield a scalpel to their own work serves as a testament to the difficulty of the craft: further reassurance that writing is hard for everyone (even them!) but that each word takes us one inch farther from the ledge.

Finally, at the end of the book you'll find a writing exercise specifically designed to correspond with each essay, giving the reader the chance to put the newly learned lessons to quick use.

I urge you not only to read this book but to write in it also. You are encouraged to scrawl on the table of contents and the inner cover. Scribble until all the blank spaces are filled and then move on to a fresh page in a fresh notebook, and on to the next after that. It is my great hope that eventually, after all the notebooks have been filled, you will discover your own path, your own voice.

And that much like my grandfather so long ago, regardless of the direction you're headed, you'll find the view exhilarating.

Marcia Aldrich

The Structure of Trouble

Some think of trouble

as difficulty, as something to be overcome. **Examples:** I'm having some trouble untying this knot. I'm experiencing some trouble getting into my kayak. I'm having some trouble getting my horse to move forward.

The assumption is that a remedy is available: the knot can be untied, you can be assisted into the kayak, the horse can be moved forward from its stopped position.

as the negative consequence of unwise or forbidden behavior. **Examples:** Pregnancy as the consequence of unprotected sex; a traffic ticket as the consequence of speeding.

Personal Example: In eighth grade, my science teacher, Mr. Samuels, warned me to stop pumping my leg. I had trouble (as in difficulty) keeping still in my seat for the whole period and I jiggled my leg *aggressively*, according to Mr. Samuels, scissor kicking, he called it. He warned me that if I didn't stop, there would be negative consequences. I didn't stop. I couldn't stop. Mr. Samuels took down the wood paddle hanging on the wall near the blackboard and paddled me in front of the class.

as when someone or something behaves in such a consistently troubling manner that she becomes synonymous with the word trouble. **Examples:** My friend Martha has a puppy who so regularly misbehaves that instead of calling the puppy by her name, Lousie, Martha says, "Here comes Trouble." Or a kitten named Trouble because he was repeatedly found caught in the toilet bowl.

as a specific event of a certain duration that causes distress, that disturbs the heretofore tranquil waters of our life. **Examples:** bad news (that can be gotten over), a fight (that will be resolved), a storm (that will pass through).

> **Question:** But what if trouble is something larger than a fight or a storm or a piece of bad news? What if it's a depth we plumb? What if it isn't an event but something that lives in the body and, like the blues, it comes upon us, it comes over us and we don't know when or if it will pass?

> Women may get the blues;
> Men are more likely to get a bullet
> Through the temple.[1]

How Trouble Feels

It feels like a headache. Even though I don't get headaches, that's what I say when it's too hard to describe what I feel like when trouble comes, when I'm heartsick and want to lie down, when I can't stand up to the day before me. A headache is an acceptable reason to lie

1. Barbara Ehrenreich, "Did Feminism Make Women Miserable?" *Salon.com*, October 15, 2009.

down in the middle of the day, or so it seems in my experience. Who says, I can't stand up anymore to her boss, her teacher, her paramour? No one who wants to keep her job. Complicated excuses or explanations that require interpretation don't cut it in the workaday world.

What You Can't Say

You can't say: *It's a blue afternoon suddenly and I've got to lie down.*

You can't say: *For some reason I can't pinpoint, I'm remembering something that happened to one of my best friends in ninth grade who rode horses with me. How one night that year, horses at the stable were left out in the pasture when they shouldn't have been, despite tornado warnings. How in the storm the horses broke out of the fenced pasture and ran as a group onto the highway where because of the storm and the dark drivers couldn't see. Some of them were hit and killed and my friend's horse was among them.*

> **Question**: I don't know why I am sometimes visited by this memory. Does the memory make me low or does my state of lowness trigger the memory? Which comes first? I never picture their deaths—just the running and the blood draining from their brains, and then my friend getting smaller and smaller, shrinking into a wizened old woman, shrinking into someone I could hardly recognize from the girl I once knew.

> **WARNING**: It will not go well for you if you say anything like this. People will think you are unbalanced and given to visitations. The untroubled mask must be fitted closely to your face at all times while in public.

What You Can Say

A literal medical condition is required. That's what people understand and accept. In my experience, females are incapacitated by migraines on a regular basis. All manner of female has employed the headache to get out of whatever she was supposed to be doing, to craft an exit.

Most Frequent Time of Visitation

No doubt this is a subjective calculation; some might say from dusk to dawn, the hours of darkness, what some people call the sinking time. But not me. I say late afternoon. At least that's when it begins to make its first appearance.

Right now as the dinner hour approaches, women are lying down all over the world. I can hear the collective sigh of mattresses as they lie down with their loneliness, with whatever fells them.

Personal History: I've only known one man to claim a headache before dinner and that was my husband, who said his head hurt after he slipped on the black ice of our driveway and hit his head so hard he knocked himself out. That's what it took for him to say he had a headache and needed to lie down. Men do other things when trouble comes upon them. But those things are not what I think about when I think about trouble. I don't get headaches; I don't know why. I'm not complaining, mind you, I just find it odd to have the quintessential female affliction pass me by.

How It Feels to Me

Imagine a line of dancers, a chorus line, all moving to the same relentless beat with no appearance of difficulty and suddenly one of the dancers falls out of step, she's a beat off, a beat slow, and then two beats, and soon she staggers out of the line altogether and has to grab hold of the velvet curtain backstage to keep from collapsing. What came over her, you ask. Who can say exactly, but she needs to go lie down immediately.

That's how it is for me. One moment I'm fine, moving in the rhythm, in the line, in the chorus, until I'm not. I call what happens a falling, a staggering, but rather than falter, my heart flutters, a kind of stuttering rhythm, like a blue moth flapping from side to side inside my chest, caught in an existential corner.

Origins

The trouble with troubled relationships is they are troubled. And when the relationship is with one's parents, and especially one's mother, and has been troubled since birth, or so it feels, then one's whole life is framed by this trouble.

Personal Backstory: My parents never spoke of the circumstances surrounding my birth. No baby pictures were taken. No baby book, where the milestones are recorded, exists. One winter evening after dinner while we were washing up the dishes, I asked my mother what she remembered about my birth. "Well," she said, taken aback by the sudden question, "you were a small baby, only five pounds, and you had to stay in the hospital for two weeks before you could come home."

"Was there anything wrong with me?"

"Nothing lasting," she said as she wiped the counter for the second time. I couldn't understand why she didn't want to tell me about my birth, why she seemed to be keeping something from me.

"Do you remember anything else?" I asked.

She said, "You weren't born as planned," and looked at me hard, as if an old anger had been stirred out of the corner. "You were two weeks past your due date and in the middle of the night my water broke."

I didn't have the foggiest idea what she meant by waters breaking. Was she being metaphorical about not being able to hold me inside her any longer? She seemed angry, angry at me. The words *plan, water breaking* were parts of a puzzle called my birth that I had to assemble.

"Anything else?"

That was it. She was done telling me the story of my birth. She hung her apron on the handle of the oven door and joined my father in the den to watch the nightly news.

My mother's defensiveness on the subject of my birth led me to believe that the day, the event, my first entrance onto the stage and into my mother's life, was complicated by emotions I didn't understand and might never understand. I came to think that from my mother's point of view my birth was a mistake and that was why all the memorializing forms were blank.

Causes (1): I sometimes think of my life as one long attempt, and failure, to right the wrong-footed relationship I've had with my mother. One strategy after another, with the same result: failure. Hoping that some miracle of understanding would occur, that the origin of the trouble between us would be exposed, worked through, and put behind us—bridges would span across broken waters, hands would meet.

> **Aside:** There is an annoying resiliency in this hopeful fantasy. Despite all evidence to the contrary, hope springs eternal that we can fix things that have gone wrong even when we don't understand why they went wrong in the first place. I can't say how many times and with what vehemence I've tried to bury this hope, cremate it and scatter its ashes, set it on a leaking vessel and shove it out to sea, kick it into the deepest hole one can dig on this earth, throw it down a bottomless well. To no avail. Turn around, and there it is, hope, fresh and potent as new-mown hay, a pasture full of it.

> Causes (2): Then there's the matter of my mother's trouble, how it affected me, how I struggled to understand it.

Repeated Scene

> In the late afternoon my mother used to retire to the bedroom to lie down on her twin bed (my parents did not sleep in the same bed; that in itself is a disturbing fact and may have contributed to my mother's malaise) whose cool mint spread was permanently unwrinkled.

> **Interruption:** I have found little to be optimistic about in the facts that my parents slept in separate beds during their whole marriage and that my mother was obsessive about keeping her bedspread unwrinkled.

Her retirement often followed on the heels of my return home from school. She'd follow me into the kitchen, where I was stealing an after-school snack, open the refrigerator door, and bend over to peer inside as if the shelves were the dimly lit walls of a cave and she had no idea what lived there. She seemed a bit frightened. She'd turn to me, with hands on her thin, jutting hips, and ask in a quivering voice, *What do you think I should make for dinner?* I would suggest a few items she regularly made—meatloaf, mustard chicken, seven-layer casserole—and all of them angered her for reasons I have struggled to understand. In a huff, she'd throw open the cabinets above the stove and look behind the boxes of crackers and cereal as if she'd discover a murder weapon. (The anger didn't last; maybe it would have been better if it had. Anger often keeps one from collapse. But as I said, her anger would subside and collapse would come.) Finding nothing, she'd put the boxes back into their places and say, "Just thinking about dinner gives me a headache. I'm going to lie down for a few minutes." Down the beige hall to her bedroom she'd pad, trouble incarnate, and then she'd close her door.

It was never a few minutes.

The other character in the drama of the repeated scene was my father.

He would arrive home from work expecting dinner to be in preparation, if not ready, and instead he would find my mother lying down.

Aside: When I hear people say that feminism makes women unhappy and it would be better to return to the good old days when men and women knew their places, I want to beat my head against the wall. They didn't live in my house where my father knew his place (he had the job, made the money, and expected to have dinner served to him by my mother or some female substitute at the end of the day) and my mother knew hers (she was supposed to oversee meals, specifically dinner). It had been decided by my parents under the watchful eye of the god of matrimony that dinner had to take place at the same time each day, at six o'clock sharp, or else. This was the meal grid.

My father never went to my mother to see what the trouble was. Instead he sat in the living room supposedly reading the paper but secretly watching the sun set over the icy fields and river curving like a question mark below our house.

Question: What was he thinking? He was probably wondering how long this latest spell of my mother's would last. Would she open the bedroom door and emerge ready to make dinner, or would she stay wrapped in her mint-green spread until morning?

On these occasions my father did not endeavor to feed himself or me, rustling up cheese and crackers, at the very least. No. He slumped in his lounge chair, looking out into the dark that had fallen, until he concluded my mother would not be putting in an appearance.

Third Character in Repeated Scene (Like Mother, Like Daughter, the Chain of Substitution)

Eventually he called me into the living room and, without any preamble, asked: *Will dinner be ready anytime soon?*

On these evenings I made a box of something, usually maca-roni and cheese, brought my father his bowl, and took my own portion into my room where I disappeared for the rest of the night. I padded heavily down the same beige hallway as my mother, trouble incarnate, following her foot impressions in the plush pile.

Conclusion of Repeated Scene

I never heard my father enter the bedroom they shared.

> **Lingering Question:** Why did my mother not think she had the wherewithal to refuse dinner, to alter the marital script so as to alleviate her anxiety? Suppose a documentary were made and the filmmaker pulled my mother aside and asked her, *What do you really think about dinner?* My mother, if she were truthful, would look into the camera and say, *I hate it!* And once she uttered those three little words, she'd say more. There might be no end to what she'd say about women and dinner and marriage and other things that troubled her. My mother never said any of these things and I don't know why.

Mystery and Manners

The next morning my mother gave some explanation for her disap-pearance. *She had a headache* was one of her usual ones. Sometimes she said, "I'm so tired," in a threadbare voice that baffled me. I couldn't understand what tired her, what made it so hard to get through the late afternoon and dinner. It seemed to me at that early age that my mother had nothing to do all day, and I envied her freedom. I couldn't fathom why my father's expectation that my mother make dinner caused her to fall apart.

As a child I did not understand the mysteries of marital relations and adult disappointment.

Even now I don't know why my mother never found something to devote herself to, something that was hers. The gap between my mother's promise and the outcome, between the talented and spirited mother I knew and the mother who decided to lie down, is a mystery I haven't solved.

But the explanation for her disappearance that unnerved me the most was when she said, "I don't feel like myself," and then looked into her coffee cup as if it might be poisoned.

Question: What did that mean? Whom did she feel like? Was she referring to a marriage as a body-snatching experience?

Trouble, Mine

Fear

I fear my heartsickness is a variation of my mother's "I don't feel like myself." When I lie down in the late afternoon, I worry that what ails me, what's come over me, is my mother. I fear that I am my mother, that I, too, am susceptible to the gap between promise and outcome, between how things should be and how things are. There's a pause, of some hours, when the machinery of my life breaks down. I don't know what to call it, this low, this trouble. My body slows down, but not my brain. My brain goes *Drive on* while I'm lying on my side, holding myself like a clenched fist, like a bud that will not open. I turn toward the sliding glass doors looking out into the backyard. Nothing moves but my eyes. They blink and blink again.

I don't know why I absorb other people's trouble, the sorrow that leaks out of car windows and suitcases at the passenger drop-off. But I do. Maybe it's because I grew up trying to understand my mother. It started young, this absorbing of trouble, taking it in, making it mine. It started with my mother.

Fall

I feel the need to lie down most in the autumn of the year. It's then that my heart feels like a sore. I feel a shifting in my chest, the way a rose, once soft and unfolding, begins to harden into a hard fist with the first frost. And the visitations begin.

Often my father stands on my front stoop in a beige and stained raincoat, the collar turned up, his glasses fogged, with an attaché case extended from his arm. I open the door and he grabs my arm and moves us through the vestibule with a sense of urgency I can't understand. He sets the attaché case on the kitchen counter and removes a slip of paper, which he waves before my face. Written there is his age and the number of times I've visited in the last ten years. One sum is large and one sum is embarrassingly small. "How much time do you think I have left?" he asks.

I leave my father in the kitchen but he follows me into the bedroom. He does not remove his raincoat, his shoes drip steadily into the carpet.

I'd like to drift off to sleep before anyone else shows up, but my mother sprawls on the bed beside me. "You called," she says. "No, I didn't call you." Just like old times, we argue while my father stands dripping and waving the slip of paper. My heart feels it can't take much more before it bursts inside my chest. When will my father trudge back to his retirement home? When will my mother return to her grave? When will the ice thaw on the river?

Question: Could it be that when my mother said she didn't feel like herself, she actually felt most like herself? That the opposite of what she said was true? On those late afternoons was the mask showing that everything was okay breaking down?

Everything wasn't okay and for a few hours, or maybe longer, she couldn't open her eyes.

It's just the opposite for me. I lie down like my mother and I want to close my eyes like my mother, but I can't. They just stay open.

Marcia Aldrich

On "The Structure of Trouble"

Fitting Function to Form

How It Began. "The Structure of Trouble" was seeded by Joy Castro's lyric essay "Grip," which deploys its title word *as* a word (verb: "to take firmly and hold fast"; noun: "a secure grasp") to shape the reader's experience.[1] Inspired by her success, I set out to write an essay likewise built around one word. I created a list of candidates (*omission, birth, minor, enough, blind, casualty, vine,* etc.), choosing *trouble* because it spoke of something essential about me whose shape and influence I could, at that point, only intuit or discern as a moving blip on a fuzzy screen.

Radar. Having picked my word, I leafed through entries in my journal. With the rough plan of an essay in mind, I might see more of what it should be by reviewing passages of rough writing, notes, good kernels of language, and so on that hadn't yet found a formal home. The journal confirmed how often the word *trouble* pops up—and with an urgent frequency in connection with my parents (as so often for me in my writing, and so often for the human race). An excerpt from the journal: "The trouble with troubled relationships is they're troubling. And when that relationship is with one's parents and has been troubled since birth, then one's life is framed by this trouble." My thinking about trouble, as this passage shows, went round and round in a circle, as

1. *Fourth Genre* 11.2 (Fall 2009): 119–20.

if my story of trouble had no exit, no end. No denouement. And this seemed a truth about my kind of trouble.

More Radar. At this same stage I heard trouble on the tip of every tongue. I couldn't go anywhere without running into it. It was leaning on a lamppost and hanging out with women in the office. I was constant witness to others' trouble or having it myself: sometimes the difference between these two didn't exist. At a teacher conference my son was called a troublemaker. I heard a man say, "The trouble with your argument is . . ." A boy whose parents were divorcing sat on the stoop across the street, in deep trouble. The trouble was that trouble was resistant to management. I nearly drowned in the material sloshing over the banks of my poor brain. I needed levees against it, a means to focus on what was mine to tell.

What I Knew. I knew my essay wasn't driven by the conventions of plot. Thinking and feeling were my mode, a different kind of story that would require a different kind of organization.

Thought. In my journal I found entries that attempt to define my trouble: "What fells me is that moment when I recognize my own precariousness in others' sorrows, when I see the gap between who I want to be and who I am, between the vision I had for my life and the life I actually live; call it disappointment, call it disillusionment, call it trouble." This passage comes out of thinking, rumination, a conversation within me about something in me, trying to cut closer to an understanding *for myself*. I wanted to get this defining pulse of thinking into the essay, and I believe it is there in the titles, the movement from section to section, and the going back around.

Aside. I have no illusions that my version is definitive—if successful, it may invite others to create their own structures of words central to their experience. I could say I was trying to get at the truth, but what troubles me may not trouble you. I was writing to arrive at a truer understanding, but that arrival is arrival at a station, where I, or someone else, can transfer trains to start another journey.

Forward. I had amassed anecdotes and recollections, most in the form of short paragraphs, and I had a tentative title: "What I Think about When I Think about Trouble." I wanted to suggest an analytic, technical approach to the subject, in defiance of its molten power.

Outline. I thought of including a Reed-Kellogg sentence diagram, then realized I didn't want *a* diagram; I wanted the analytical spirit of diagramming to be represented in the essay's form. I set off to embody that idea by treating the pieces of writing I had assembled as elements in a formal outline. In a draft quite close to the final version, there was an A, B1, B2, B2a, B2b sort of format, with letters and numbers, but I gave that up because the material wasn't that orderly. So I settled on headings and indents to carry the implication (the illusion) of analytical precision. That called for a different title for the essay, a simple description of it.

The outline form helps decenter the I and disperse it into multiple roles or selves. At points in the essay I am an inquisitor; I resist patterns I myself describe, I dispense advice. At all points I am troubling the proceedings. The outline structure allows me the mobility to take different positions from which to complicate my thinking on the subject. I am outlining the structure of trouble, but more importantly I am meeting myself along the way.

Word Cloud. Near the end of the writing I became aware of word clouds, graphic representations of the frequency of terms in text. They are another version of precision, now built out of individual words rather than paragraphs. In my cloud the largest word, larger than *trouble* itself, is *mother*. Trouble is born out of her, seeded by her. And within the cloud are other words that contain a whole treatise on the word *trouble*.

parents   DOOR   bedroom

hours   hard   TROUBLE night

eyes keeping   home   make

repeated   retirement   stop   never
failure   marriage

Monica Berlin

The Eighteenth Week

The morning after they find out something is wrong, the house fills up with strangers. It's just bad timing, really, that they'd scheduled all the maintenance and repairmen to come on the same Wednesday—after all, why not get everything taken care of at once—but when the doorbell starts ringing just after eight o'clock, just after her husband's left for the office, she's startled by how much care this old house needs. By noon, eleven men are working in different rooms on separate tasks. If she weren't so devastated, she knows she could find humor here; she'd imagine an episode of I Love Lucy, the small Ricardo apartment filling with coveralls. But these high ceilings do not echo with Cuban song, and her sudden grief carries too much weight.

She barely shows yet, unless you know her well enough to have noticed the slightest curve at her waist, the tightening fabric across her chest, the graying skin just below her eyes, and so when she answers the door she cannot quite say, My baby might be dying. Cannot quite say, It could be so bad I might have to wish the baby dead. Cannot announce to any of these men, I want to die. Instead she says, Of course, this way.

They all know each other, have always worked together. At the screen door no one remembers not to let slam, they chat about business, their wives, plans for lunch. The plumbers joke about which of their grandfathers would have installed the toilet. The first time the door snaps shut, the carpenter announces, You just can't get a door like this anymore. Even as he's the one who lets it go the hardest, he promises to bring a plane tomorrow to ease the banging. These men, she thinks, these men know heartache. The carpenter — now sanding down plaster in the first-floor bathroom, tracking dust in and out, that carpenter, retired fifteen years from the factory, now just a shell of a building on the west side of town, the one that had boarded-up windows and doors when it packed up, the one that left on a light only so everyone could find their way out — is listening to the electrician talk about his sons in the desert, how one of their jobs is to sweep for improvisational roadside bombs, how the other stands at a checkpoint where civilians wait to pass. She thinks about this man's children keeping track, looking carefully, and all those ordinary people fidgeting with documentation, going in and coming out, every hour of the day, their eyes focused on nothing, their heads turned down.

Back in bed, pretending the house is just hers again, she turns on her left side, curled away, practicing words she isn't sure she'll be able to say. Words like, We lost the baby, even though it might be a lie. It might have to be more accurate to say, We had to lose the baby. But the construction is awkward, she knows. Nothing fits. She tries each phrase on, over and over, the way a month ago in the overpriced maternity boutique she had velcroed that round pillow around her waist before pulling on shirts too wide, too swingy, over her head. She couldn't imagine how her body would fill them.

She hears the men chattering to each other. One patches an old plaster wall. Another services the water heater, with its slow dribble, its too-small basin. Ashamed now, she remembers, months ago, how she had hoped for a flood so they could afford to replace everything. Who wishes for a flood? Someone changes the air filter on the furnace. Someone measures the length of the floor between pipes. If she didn't know better, everything they said would sound like a euphemism: their plumbing problems, their troubled wiring, the sloppy mistakes made before they knew better.

The day before this invasion, she and her husband had seen the bridge of the baby's nose, the long line of its spine—perfectly arched—and she had counted its ribs. Her husband asked the sonographer questions. Between answers—Yes, two ears. Yes, two eyes. Yes—she held her breath. When they had heard its heartbeat they forgot to ask anything else, and although the room filled with what they thought was wonder, she knows now that the technician had seen something wrong, had willed them silent by turning on the machine's sound, had distracted them while she looked closely at something they wouldn't have been able to decipher. They were sent back into the waiting room, clutching their foggy, strange pictures.

Again, then, they were sounding out names, playing a game that had been theirs longer than they had talked with any seriousness about having a child. The last few weeks, her husband started calling the baby Time. He laughed about it, this acronym for Thing: It Must Eat, but it had stuck. Because she had never been someone to eat more than once a day and now she was packing sandwiches to take to the office, small plastic bags with carrots for an afternoon snack, saltines wrapped in her purse, he thought it would make her feel better about the hunger, blaming it on this little speck of a body, making it not about her. At first, it seemed funny. He would ask, What's Time doing? Where's Time now? One morning just before this eighteenth week, half asleep, she had said, What if Time isn't right? She had said, What if Time disappears?

The men ring the bell out of politeness, despite the front door being wide open for them to come in and out, bang in and out, traipsing mud in from last night's rain. Between the metallic ring and the sound their boots make along the pine floors, she can't sleep. Instead, she keeps replaying her midwife explaining, If the specialist says we need to terminate—. She wonders at the pronoun, the verb, this woman's calm. She thinks about after, the word terminate choking in her throat, her husband holding her hand, and how the midwife had shown them out a back door—to give them privacy, she had said—but how they had passed through a large room where she'd never been before, a chair lowered to the floor and everything newly scrubbed clean. Weren't they supposed to see that room, supposed to be reassured that sometimes procedures have to happen and that they happen in the same place and with the same people with whom you also share these other kinds of days, these other turning points, everything becoming routine? Maybe, too, the midwife hadn't wanted to scare the others, all those women flipping through magazines, full, hopeful, waiting their turn.

Someone trips the breaker, and for a minute, the house is dead still. When the power comes back, she's holding her breath, listening for the men, waiting for something to catch. She wonders why she heeded the recommendation to wait on the first ultrasound. Why had they waited until after she'd packed up her smaller clothes, after she'd wrapped her more delicate bras in tissue, after they'd picked out a rocking chair? She had just told her colleagues she'd be taking some time off, practiced the words *maternity* and *leave* and *expecting* for weeks before she said them aloud. How would she walk it back? Would she be expected to? They had told their families at week twelve, her sister whispering between clenched teeth, Don't say anything else until the ultrasound, until you see it—there, again, the pronoun inexact, imprecise, unavoidable. To reassure her, she had told her sister then that she'd felt its heartbeat weeks ago, lying still on her back—which she wouldn't be able to do much longer—in the deepest quiet of the night, her husband beside her. On the other end of the line, her sister stayed quiet. Maybe she had been wrong, swearing she felt its heart. Why had they waited until the eighteenth week? What was safer about it? Christ, they had fallen in love with each other all over again, every day suddenly playful, secret. They had even let themselves fall in love with the baby, the idea of the baby. It had just started its fluttering, too. She knew that much wasn't imagined. It was moving inside her, like thin wings flapping against the walls of her, so slight, still half abstraction.

They don't make 'em like this anymore, each of them says, clomping along the floorboards. She's sure they say this every time, in every home that lines the northern streets of town. It's endearing, really, their admiration for houses. She's still awed, too, after all these years: the craftsmanship, each curve, the character upheld in the integrity of each building, in the fingerprints left over time. So much personality, each of them says as they let slam the wooden door, their necks craning up, their eyes surveying. Funny little house, another says. What a quirky place. In bed, listening, she nods.

The woman who had the house built, apparently, held so firmly to superstition that she demanded the house believe it too. Afraid of ghosts, certain they'd come to the front door and ask to be invited in, she had the builder make the foyer a spirit room, a small trapezoid with a near-floor-to-ceiling mirror facing the street, so that if a ghost did come to the front glass door to knock, it would see its reflection in the mirror and be scared away. Framed by windows on either side of the door, a wall of beveled glass, and on the two smaller sides of the room, matching wooden doors that hid the twin living rooms—one a sitting room and the other a parlor—that room, that small room, convinced her this had to be the house where they'd grow old together. She couldn't have known the sound that screen door would make, or that in winter the spirit room would frost over, or that bad luck wouldn't always stand on the porch, facing itself, to ring the bell. Still, she had never loved anywhere more. The house's symmetry, how it repeated itself on either side, was a marvel to her. Sometimes she imagined folding the house in half and pressing one side against the other, flattening it out, matching up its edges, unfolding it another way. Today, waiting for the men to finish, she starts counting doors and thresholds, windows, considers the few places where the pattern of the house breaks. She wonders why such inconsistencies might have been acceptable for the woman who believed, so strongly, in the fact of repetition.

She remembers hearing that when spinning a web, some spiders use their legs as a way to measure the silken threads, to make it even. She wonders why all spiders didn't do this. She wonders if the woman who had this house built watched those orb spiders in the garden stretch out a limb to make their perfect webs. She thinks about her body making this baby, about how her body knows what to do but sometimes doesn't. And she thinks about the symmetry of parts, the body trying to replicate itself in miniature. Behind her bedroom wall, where the roofline curves, the electrician talks to someone else about circuitry—such a beautiful word—even though this morning, there is only their purposefulness. To fix the things that can be fixed and replace what cannot.

Monica Berlin

On "The Eighteenth Week"

On Point of View

Shortly after her son was born, she kept hearing what would become the last two sentences of "The Eighteenth Week." She hadn't written fiction in many years and wrongly assumed those words—not even a proper sentence yet—had brought the genre back to her. Another thing was happening around the same time: her arms never empty, her hands never *not* holding him, she learned to write by memory. Shaping a line or sentence in her mouth, she learned each word by heart until she found herself, late night, in front of the computer. Those drafty things—sometimes poems, sometimes short prose pieces—in which her son is clearly present explored the early months of parenting and raised, for her, the ethical questions at stake in writing about someone who didn't ask to be written about any more than he had asked to be born, whose privacy should be his own and whose privacy she'd protected fiercely from the start. Committed to never writing anything that would later cause him discomfort or heartache, that would lead to embarrassment or shame, she knew she owed him, and herself, the same respect and care she believed she'd always used to tend to her subject matter. That same responsibility.

Still, she couldn't shake the echo of those earliest words, those fragments she'd repeat while she rocked her son or held him, asleep, against her chest. The earliest version of the opening sentence was, "The morning after, the house fills up with strangers." The end: "Even though this morning, there is only their purposefulness. To fix the things that can be fixed and replace what cannot." Yet, for all her recitations, those words remained generic in their point of view. She knew, from the start, that "their purposefulness" referred to the strangers, to the workers and repairmen who had convened on her house the morning after that terrible ultrasound. But what to do about whose house it was? How to navigate the necessity of these strangers, their task-driven purposefulness, their simultaneous humanity and oblivion to the woman in whose house they worked?

In trying to answer these questions, she discovered that the story she wanted to write wasn't actually about her son, who hadn't yet been born in the present of what would become "The Eighteenth Week." Lost from the story she needed to tell, too, was the fact that she found out on the day in which the essay is set that she was carrying was a boy. Only when elements of how to refer to the unborn child became a very real dilemma of the piece's protagonist—who was, of course, her—did she reconcile the fact that she'd been so overcome with fear on the day of the ultrasound that she had forgotten all those grainy photos showed: the bridge of his nose, the curve of his spine, him floating there, and then, too, *herself*, a way of seeing herself she'd never seen before.

Recalling her own surprise at seeing those sonogram images, she began to consider how little of ourselves we see or let others see. In this way it occurred to her that those workmen in her house couldn't have known the heartache of those hours, just as she couldn't know theirs, just as each of them might not have acknowledged, fully, their own. In these ways the *real* craft of the piece came about in the fall of 2008, four years after the birth of her son, when a friend was telling her about a conversation he'd overheard: two strangers discussing their grown children deployed in Iraq. He'd eavesdropped only the smallest snip of a conversation, and certainly his recounting of it was longer than what he'd heard. Listening hard to her friend, she realized the ways all of us must balance the potential grief of our lives with the *going on* of our lives.

She hadn't, in early drafts of "The Eighteenth Week," considered those men, their lives. She had thought only about herself, what I was struggling with and through. She needed some distance from I; she needed to be able to utilize a fictive third, to be able to pull back in order to hear what those men might've said to one another. The truth, too: on that day, so delirious with sadness, she'd have never heard a word any of those men said to one another. She never would've thought about them. Fictive elements of "The Eighteenth Week" bear themselves out in her allowing herself, all those years later, to hear them—to complicate their lives with the truths of *every* life, even if the details themselves are altered. True to the essay, beyond what she experienced, is that we are always learning to let go, to grieve for the loss of another, to empathize with another if we allow ourselves to recognize *not* that it wasn't us—not to be grateful that it wasn't us—but instead to acknowledge that every grief is equal. Every sadness potent, portent, present, real.

In the end, "The Eighteenth Week" is an essay not because it's any truer than it would've been as a short story but because that's what she called it. Making it, she sought the transformative experience of the *lyric* I but turned toward the fictive *she* to enable the narrative to turn, to overhear something within range, just behind the bedroom wall, and essentially, too, to be able to hide behind that *she* as a way to protect her little boy from a certain future over which he has little control. This device, a sleight of hand, really, is one she recognized all along. But choice of point of view, however rhetorical a strategy, as it is here, allowed her the ability to attend to others as it simultaneously enabled her to mourn what her body did to the body of the one who would become her child. More, it allowed her to step outside of her experience long enough to consider the ways our bodies teach us through replication and miniature, through our own foreignness and familiarity, through symmetrical consideration of even the most seemingly unmeasurable things. When we can look toward another, consider another, as we simultaneously consider our self, we can find space inclusive enough for disclosure, empathy, and revelation.

Eula Biss

Time and Distance Overcome

"Of what use is such an invention?" the *New York World* asked shortly after Alexander Graham Bell first demonstrated his telephone in 1876. The world was not waiting for the telephone.

Bell's financial backers asked him not to work on his new invention because it seemed too dubious an investment. The idea on which the telephone depended—the idea that every home in the country could be connected with a vast network of wires suspended from poles set an average of one hundred feet apart—seemed far more unlikely than the idea that the human voice could be transmitted through a wire.

Even now it is an impossible idea, that we are all connected, all of us.

"At the present time we have a perfect network of gas pipes and water pipes throughout our large cities," Bell wrote to his business partners in defense of his idea. "We have main pipes laid under the streets communicating by side pipes with the various dwellings. . . . In a similar manner it is conceivable that cables of telephone wires could be laid under ground, or suspended overhead, communicating by branch wires with private dwellings, counting houses, shops, manufactories, etc., uniting them through the main cable."

Imagine the mind that could imagine this. That could see us joined by one branching cable. This was the mind of a man who wanted to invent, more than the telephone, a machine that would allow the deaf to hear.

For a short time the telephone was little more than a novelty. For twenty-five cents you could see it demonstrated by Bell himself, in a church, along with singing and recitations by local talent. From some distance away, Bell would receive a call from "the invisible Mr. Watson." Then the telephone became a plaything of the rich. A Boston banker paid for a private line between his office and his home so that he could let his family know exactly when he would be home for dinner.

Mark Twain was among the first Americans to own a telephone, but he wasn't completely taken with the device. "The human voice carries entirely too far as it is," he remarked.

By 1889, the *New York Times* was reporting a "War on Telephone Poles." Wherever telephone companies were erecting poles, homeowners and business owners were sawing them down, or defending their sidewalks with rifles.

Property owners in Red Bank, New Jersey, threatened to tar and feather the workers putting up telephone poles. A judge granted a group of homeowners an injunction to prevent the telephone company from erecting any new poles. Another judge found that a man who had cut down a pole because it was "obnoxious" was not guilty of malicious mischief.

Telephone poles, newspaper editorials complained, were an urban blight. The poles carried a wire for each telephone—sometimes hundreds of wires. And in some places there were also telegraph wires, power lines, and trolley cables. The sky was netted with wires.

The war on telephone poles was fueled, in part, by that terribly American concern for private property, and a reluctance to surrender it for a shared utility. And then there was a fierce sense of aesthetics, an obsession with purity, a dislike for the way the poles and wires marred a landscape that those other new inventions, skyscrapers and barbed wire, were just beginning to complicate. And then perhaps there was also a fear that distance, as it had always been known and measured, was collapsing.

The city council in Sioux Falls, South Dakota, ordered policemen to cut down all the telephone poles in town. And the mayor of Oshkosh, Wisconsin, ordered the police chief and the fire department to chop down the telephone poles there. Only one pole was chopped down before the telephone men climbed all the poles along the line, preventing any more chopping. Soon, Bell Telephone Company began stationing a man at the top of each pole as soon as it had been set, until enough poles had been set to string a wire between them, at which point it became a misdemeanor to interfere with the poles. Even so, a constable cut down two poles holding forty or fifty wires. And a homeowner sawed down a recently wired pole, then fled from police. The owner of a cannery ordered his workers to throw dirt back into the hole the telephone company was digging in front of his building. His men threw the dirt back in as fast as the telephone workers could dig it out. Then he sent out a team with a load of stones to dump into the hole. Eventually, the pole was erected on the other side of the street.

Despite the war on telephone poles, it would take only four years after Bell's first public demonstration of the telephone for every town of more than ten thousand people to be wired, although many towns were wired only to themselves. By the turn of the century, there were more telephones than bathtubs in America.

"Time and dist. overcome," read an early advertisement for the telephone. Rutherford B. Hayes pronounced the installation of a telephone in the White House "one of the greatest events since creation." The telephone, Thomas Edison declared, "annihilated time and space, and brought the human family in closer touch."

———

In 1898, in Lake Cormorant, Mississippi, a black man was hanged from a telephone pole. And in Weir City, Kansas. And in Brookhaven, Mississippi. And in Tulsa, Oklahoma, where the hanged man was riddled with bullets. In Danville, Illinois, a black man's throat was slit, and his dead body was strung up on a telephone pole. Two black men were hanged from a telephone pole in Lewisburg, West Virginia. And two in Hempstead, Texas, where one man was dragged out of the courtroom by a mob, and another was dragged out of jail.

A black man was hanged from a telephone pole in Belleville, Illinois, where a fire was set at the base of the pole and the man was cut down half-alive, covered in coal oil, and burned. While his body was burning the mob beat it with clubs and cut it to pieces.

Lynching, the first scholar of the subject determined, is an American invention. Lynching from bridges, from arches, from trees standing alone in fields, from trees in front of the county courthouse, from trees used as public billboards, from trees barely able to support the weight of a man, from telephone poles, from street lamps, and from poles erected solely for that purpose. From the middle of the nineteenth century to the middle of the twentieth century black men were lynched for crimes real and imagined, for whistles, for rumors, for "disputing with a white man," for "unpopularity," for "asking a white woman in marriage," for "peeping in a window."

The children's game of telephone depends on the fact that a message passed quietly from one ear to another to another will get distorted at some point along the line.

More than two hundred antilynching bills were introduced in the U.S. Congress during the twentieth century, but none were passed. Seven presidents lobbied for antilynching legislation, and the House of Representatives passed three separate measures, each of which was blocked by the Senate.

In Pine Bluff, Arkansas, a black man charged with kicking a white girl was hanged from a telephone pole. In Longview, Texas, a black man accused of attacking a white woman was hanged from a telephone pole. In Greenville, Mississippi, a black man accused of attacking a white telephone operator was hanged from a telephone pole. "The negro only asked time to pray." In Purcell, Oklahoma, a black man accused of attacking a white woman was tied to a telephone pole and burned. "Men and women in automobiles stood up to watch him die."

The poles, of course, were not to blame. It was only coincidence that they became convenient as gallows, because they were tall and straight, with a crossbar, and because they stood in public places. And it was only coincidence that the telephone poles so closely resembled crucifixes.

Early telephone calls were full of noise. "Such a jangle of meaningless noises had never been heard by human ears," Herbert Casson wrote in his 1910 *History of the Telephone*. "There were spluttering and bubbling, jerking and rasping, whistling and screaming."

In Shreveport, Louisiana, a black man charged with attacking a white girl was hanged from a telephone pole. "A knife was left sticking in the body." In Cumming, Georgia, a black man accused of assaulting a white girl was shot repeatedly, then hanged from a telephone pole. In Waco, Texas, a black man convicted of killing a white woman was taken from the courtroom by a mob and burned, then his charred body was hanged from a telephone pole.

A postcard was made from the photo of a burned man hanging from a telephone pole in Texas, his legs broken off below the knee and his arms curled up and blackened. Postcards of lynchings were sent out as greetings and warnings until 1908, when the postmaster general declared them unmailable. "This is the barbecue we had last night," reads one.

"If we are to die," W. E. B. DuBois wrote in 1911, "in God's name let us not perish like bales of hay." And "if we must die," Claude McKay wrote ten years later, "let it not be like hogs."

In Pittsburg, Kansas, a black man was hanged from a telephone pole, cut down, burned, shot, and stoned with bricks. "At first the negro was defiant," the *New York Times* reported, "but just before he was hanged he begged hard for his life."

In the photographs, the bodies of the men lynched from telephone poles are silhouetted against the sky. Sometimes two men to a pole, hanging above the buildings of a town. Sometimes three. They hang like flags in still air.

In Cumberland, Maryland, a mob used a telephone pole as a battering ram to break into the jail where a black man charged with the murder of a policeman was being held. They kicked him to death, then fired twenty shots into his head. They wanted to burn his body, but a minister asked them not to.

The lynchings happened everywhere, in all but four states. From shortly before the invention of the telephone to long after the first trans-Atlantic call. More in the South, and more in rural areas. In the cities and in the North, there were race riots.

Riots in Cincinnati, New Orleans, Memphis, New York, Atlanta, Philadelphia, Houston . . .

During the race riots that destroyed the black section of Springfield, Ohio, a black man was shot and hanged from a telephone pole.

During the race riots that set fire to East St. Louis and forced five hundred black people to flee their homes, a black man was hanged from a telephone pole. The rope broke and his body fell into the gutter. "Negros are lying in the gutters every few feet in some places," read the newspaper account.

In 1921, the year before Bell died, four companies of the National Guard were called out to end a race war in Tulsa that began when a white woman accused a black man of rape. Bell had lived to complete the first call from New York to San Francisco, which required 14,000 miles of copper wire and 130,000 telephone poles.

––––––

My grandfather was a lineman. He broke his back when a telephone pole fell. "Smashed him onto the road," my father says.

When I was young, I believed that the arc and swoop of telephone wires along the roadways was beautiful. I believed that the telephone poles, with their transformers catching the evening sun, were glorious. I believed my father when he said, "My dad could raise a pole by himself." And I believed that the telephone itself was a miracle.

Now, I tell my sister, these poles, these wires, do not look the same to me. Nothing is innocent, my sister reminds me. But nothing, I would like to think, remains unrepentant.

One summer, heavy rains fell in Nebraska and some green telephone poles grew small leafy branches.

Eula Biss

On "Time and Distance Overcome"

The Rewards of Research

"Time and Distance Overcome" found its form through my effort to reproduce my research experience for the reader. I began my research for this essay by searching for every instance of the phrase telephone pole in the New York Times from 1880 to 1920, which resulted in 370 articles. I was planning to write an essay about telephone poles and telephones, a subject I hoped to maneuver into a metaphor for collective efforts to stay in touch. I was not planning to write an essay about lynchings, but as I read through the articles produced by my search I discovered that there was a significant period of time in which telephone poles were mentioned in the Times most often when someone had been hanged from one. After reading an article headlined "Colored Scoundrel Lynched," and then another headlined "Mississippi Negro Lynched," and then another headlined "Texas Negro Lynched," I searched for every instance of the word lynched in the New York Times from 1880 to 1920, which resulted in 2,354 articles.

I should not have been surprised—the time period I was searching was the Jim Crow era, and I knew as well as any student of American history knows what happened during Jim Crow. But knowing did not prepare me for the experience of reading one article after another, lynching after lynching, in which the same grotesque details—the stoning of the hanged man, the knifing of the hanged man, the burning of his body, the cutting to pieces of the charred corpse—were repeated over and over in a sickeningly relentless litany.

And so the body and bulk of my essay became a litany, a list, of lynchings from telephone poles. In its anaphora and repeated patterns and deliberate redundancy this essay shares its strategies with the tradition of poetic and liturgical litanies. But my purpose in using these devices was not to create lovely cadences and a rhythmic structure so much as it was to create a brutally repetitive experience for the reader. Litanies can be lulling and comforting, but that was not the aspect of the litany I wanted to work with—I wanted a relentless, uncomfortable repetition.

In an effort to heighten the discomfort of this litany, I set it inside a light, somewhat humorous frame so the reader might feel as unsettled as I felt in my research. I returned to the subject matter of that frame—the invention of the telephone—at the end of the essay, but all the lightness, of course, was gone then. If this essay shares one edge with poetry, it also shares one with personal essay, and a feature of that tradition—the overt use of the first person—appears only here, in the last section of the essay. Why the first person is necessary here at the end is still somewhat mysterious to me, but that seemed to be what the essay demanded. Joan Didion has a short essay, "Marrying Absurd," in which she uses the first person only in the last paragraph, and John McPhee has a sixty-thousand-word essay, "The Deltoid Pumpkin Seed," in which he originally used the pronoun I only once (he added a couple more instances at his editor's insistence). Those two writers, themselves working in a hybrid of journalism and personal essay, provided a helpful model for my hybridization.

Ryan Boudinot

An Essay and a Story
about Mötley Crüe

Part 1: My Favorite Band in Seventh Grade

I became a fan of Mötley Crüe around their album *Shout at the Devil*. Check out those fellows on the cover, sporting their sadomasochism-inspired duds! Between the albums *Shout at the Devil* and *Theatre of Pain*, the Crüe changed their wardrobe, glamming it up in spandex and polka dots. I preferred the bondage gear Mötley Crüe much better. I had Mötley Crüe posters all over my room, and in most of them their expressions could have been described as "kissy face" or "bowel movement."

This was around the time I started receiving flyers in the mail for something called Doug Marks's Metal Method. Doug Marks was a musician in Los Angeles who advertised his guitar lesson tapes and booklets in the classifieds sections of heavy metal magazines like *Circus*, *Metal Edge*, and *Hit Parader*. These ads were often the best part of the magazine. My favorites were the ones soliciting musicians to join bands, typically ending in the words "Hair a must." The deal with Doug Marks was you bought X number of lessons and you'd learn to shred like the pros. In his flyers Mr. Marks spoke enthusiastically of "licks" and "riffs" and cited a number of professional musicians as advocates of his program, including members of Mötley Crüe. The Metal Method flyers were illustrated with pen-and-ink drawings, mostly of Doug himself, scowling in a metal attitude with a Gibson flying-V.

Holy crap, I just Googled "Doug Marks Metal Method" and he's still at it! Check him out at metalmethod.com. Hair, it appears, is still a must.

So one day I taped a Metal Method drawing of Mötley Crüe's Nikki Sixx to the inside of my locker at Conway Middle School. I thought it looked cool. In the drawing Mr. Sixx was biting down on what appears to be a concert ticket, with the word "Crüe" written on it. I was admiring it when an eighth grader, Zach Butler, walked by and said, "Crüe *sucks*." I quickly took down the drawing and kept my Mötley Crüe fandom to myself.

While I struggled with pre-algebra, Mötley Crüe hit the road to conquer the world, get blowjobs. I begged my parents to allow me to attend a Crüe concert but was firmly denied. The metal magazines promised an orgasmic show, louder than standing next to a jet engine. The band would play on a set designed to look like the gigantic spread legs of a woman. At the beginning of the show they would emerge, like babies, from the vagina. Tommy Lee would play drums upside down in a cage that hovered over the audience. There would be pyrotechnics and confetti cannons. Licks and riffs would flow like sweet nectar. I longed to raise my arms in the devil horns salute and purchase the tour's collectible tank top. I studied the band's tour itinerary. They'd be playing Seattle one night, Vancouver the next. I wondered if their pornography would get confiscated at the Canadian border again. It occurred to me that they would be transported via bus. In fact, Mötley Crüe would be driving to Vancouver on Interstate 5, *mere feet from my house.*

What if their bus broke down and they needed to use our phone?

Part 2: The Day Mötley Crüe's Bus Broke Down and They Needed to Use Our Phone

It was my responsibility to fetch wood for the two stoves that heated our home. Whenever a windstorm knocked down a tree on our seven acres my dad jumped at the chance to use his chain saw, buzzing the alder or Doug fir into segments, splitting and stacking the cordwood next to the sheep shed. We used a wheeled bin to haul wood from the pile to our back porch. One afternoon after hauling wood up to the house, my tank top covered in bits of sawdust and green smears of moss, I heard my mother talking to someone at the front door. Guess who it was.

Mötley Crüe.

I recognized them instantly. Vince Neil wore fingerless white leather gloves and a gold pentagram medallion over his see-through pink top. Black-clad Mick Marrs stood, Stratocaster in hand, absentmindedly soloing. Tommy Lee and Nicky Sixx wore a leather jockstrap and a black-and-white-polka-dot Spandex body suit, respectively. Tommy Lee also held a gas can.

"Our bus broke down on the freeway," Vince Neil said. "We were wondering if you folks might have some gas we could buy so we can make it to the closest service station."

My dad appeared, wearing the outfit I will always fondly associate with him—boots, blue jeans, a gray sweatshirt, work gloves, and the blue stocking cap my mom knitted from our sheep's wool. He had been out clearing brush, his favorite pastime, and he looked both tired and invigorated. His routine at this point would have been to take a shower and watch *The Wonderful World of Disney* with me; he hadn't counted on helping strangers in need. But these were no regular strangers, like the elderly men who occasionally showed up on our doorstep smelling of butterscotch candy and complaining of car trouble. These were multimillionaire rock stars who'd survived heroin overdoses and stuck their penises in breakfast burritos to hide the smell of other vaginas from their girlfriends. This last part I learned years later from *The Dirt: Confessions of the World's Most Notorious Rock Band*. Now, though, they needed gas.

"You can use our lawnmower gas," I said, trembling.

"That would be really cool of you," Nikki Sixx said. "We'd really appreciate that."

I led them through the house toward the back yard. Before we made it outside, they passed the open door of my bedroom. Every square inch of wall space was covered with posters and pictures of heavy metal musicians posing menacingly or captured mid-lick in concert. On the wall by my loft bed hung several posters of the men who now stood beside me. They nodded approvingly.

"You've got killer taste in music," Tommy Lee said.

"Mind if we sign our posters?" said Mick Marrs.

I gave them a pen and one by one they climbed the ladder of my loft bed and inscribed their likenesses with their awesome signatures. Nikki Sixx even drew some devil horns on the picture of him posing with a bottle of Jack Daniels.

Vince Neil picked up my copy of Stephen King's *The Stand* and had a seat on my weight bench. "Is this any good?" he said.

"It's his best book, definitely," I said.

"I'll have to pick it up next time I'm at Waldenbooks."

"Here, have my copy," I said.

"You sure? Are you finished with it?"

"I've read it twice already," I said.

"So cool of you. I'll make sure to fix you up with some T-shirts back at the bus."

Outside I showed the band to our tool shed. The sheep hustled to their barn, mistakenly believing they were about to be fed.

"Have you guys ever fucked a sheep?" Tommy Lee said. "Like on a dare?"

Nikki Sixx guffawed and Vince Neil rolled his eyes as if to say, *What's with my crazy drummer?* Mick Marrs looked quietly at the ground.

Gas in hand, we repaired to their tour bus. It was so killer. On the side were painted the comedy/tragedy masks from the *Theatre of Pain* album cover. As gawking motorists honked and raised the devil horn salute in appreciation, we ascended the stairs into this smoky lair of rock. Can you imagine for a moment what it's like for a twelve-year-old heavy metal maniac to step within the sacred circle of the very gods to whom he is subservient? I'll bet you can't. The interior of the bus reminded me of the motor home we rented one time to take a trip to the Olympic peninsula, though I don't remember any groupies in garter belts in that motor home, that's for sure. There were grizzled, tattooed roadies playing video games and doing lines of coke off the Formica table. If you've ever wondered how many naked people can fit inside of one those tour bus bathrooms I can tell you with utter confidence: ten.

The Crüe were magnanimous hosts, loading me up with tour schwag—posters, lanyards, cut-off tees. I declined their offer of cocaine and marijuana, using the peer-pressure skills I'd learned in health class. "No thank you," I said, "I would prefer not to at this time."

"Suit yourself," Nikki Sixx said, setting up his works.

"So there's a Texaco just down the hill," I said as Tommy Lee returned from pouring the gas in the tank. "They've got really good jo-jos."

The nonplussed, middle-aged bus driver tried to start the bus, but no go.

"It ain't the gas that's the problem," the driver said. "I think it's the alternator."

My eyes still wide with all the groupie/drug/video game action going down, I suggested that they use my family's phone to call a tow truck. Dejected, the Crüe followed me back to the house, where my mom had begun preparing my favorite meal—French dip sandwiches.

"That smells delicious," Mick Marrs said.

"I've got plenty for the whole band if you want to stay for din-din," my mom said.

"Are you sure?" Tommy Lee said. "We wouldn't want you to go out of your way."

My mother shrugged. "I'll just fix more meat."

One of the qualities I most admire in my parents is their hospitality and the ease with which they make new friends. They were always inviting my friends to come along with us on vacation and hosting various peripheral acquaintances for Thanksgiving. Not only did they invite Mötley Crüe to have dinner with us, they extended the invitation to their groupies and roadies as well. Twenty-seven people in all crowded into our house, their chains jangling, smelling of noxious perfumes and cigarette smoke. And my folks, bless 'em, didn't blink an eye. My dad had plenty of questions for the roadies about how exactly such a big production is erected and torn down night after night. The groupies warmly complimented my mom's macramé wall hangings, which featured the creative use of driftwood and beads. Nikki Sixx nodded off into an opiate slumber. My brother, dropped off from his day camp, immediately hit it off with the band, amusing them with his wily Mad Libs. My sister woke up from her nap, took one look at our guests, and burst into tears.

"This au jus is delicious," Vince Neil said. "I'm going to have to get the recipe."

My mom laughed. "Oh, it's just a Lowry's packet."

The bus driver appeared, rubbing his sweaty bald head. "The mechanics took one look at the bus and said it's a goner," he said.

Tommy Lee quickly got on the phone and called someone in LA. "What the fuck, Jerry? Why the fuck do we have to ride around in a shitty-ass unreliable fucking bus? And while I'm at it, I heard that Twisted Sister is touring in a fucking jet! A jet, motherfucker!"

"You guys can stay here if you need to," I said. My dad shot me a quick look, then shrugged. Why not?

That night Mötley Crüe and their personnel spread out on camping pads and inflatable mattresses around the house. My dad laid down the rules. "Ladies in the living room, guys in the family room. Lights out at ten, we've got a big day ahead of us tomorrow. Mr. Sixx, I'm going to have to ask that you indulge your narcotic habit elsewhere. This is my house and you'll observe my rules. That goes for drinking, too."

"No problem, Mr. Boudinot," Nikki Sixx said. "We're just thankful we have a place to lay our heads tonight."

"You guys have been nothing but generous," Tommy Lee said, brushing away a young blonde lady who was trying to untie his leather pants.

Mick Marrs and Vince Neil crashed in my room that night. I laid awake in my loft bed, unable to fathom that the same guys who performed "Piece of Your Action" were now curled up in their PJs on my floor. Just when I thought they were asleep, Mick said, "Hey Vince?"

"Yeah, Mick?"

"What's the weirdest thing you've ever snorted?"

Vince was quiet a moment. "I guess talcum powder. What about you?"

"I guess I haven't really snorted anything weird. Just coke, mostly. No wait, I snorted vomit one time."

"Remember when we were on tour with Ozzy and he snorted a line of live ants?"

Mick laughed. "I'd forgotten that. I thought Nikki was the one who snorted the ants."

"Maybe it was," Vince said. "Hey Ryan, what's the weirdest thing you ever snorted?"

"My friend Matt dared me to snort some of the flavor dust from a Pixie Stick once," I said.

"That's fucked up," Mick said.

"You're crazy," Vince said. I declined to tell them that I had refused the dare and been called a pussy, but it still felt good to have Mötley

Crüe members think I was wildly snorting things intended only for oral pleasure.

Then, around three in the morning, wouldn't you know it, an orgy got started in the living room. A guitar tech had commandeered the stereo and was cranking my *Star Wars and Other Galactic Funk* album loud. I peeked in and discovered groupies bouncing on the laps of roadies on the very couch where we posed for our yearly Christmas picture. My dad, bleary eyed and grouchy, stomped through the kitchen and confronted the Dionysian display. "What the hell do you people think you're doing? It's three o'clock in the damn morning!"

Sheepishly, the groupies dismounted, the roadies apologized and slipped LPs of *Whipped Cream and Other Delights* and *Jazzercise Essentials* back on the shelf, and the members of my favorite rock band commanded everyone to head back to the bus. On the way out, Vince winked at me and gave me a soft punch on the shoulder, "Watch out for the Pixie Stick dust, kid."

The next morning a tow truck arrived and hauled the *Theatre of Pain* bus away. I stood on the frontage road, waving to these men who had filled my Sony Walkman with dreams. Sure, it saddened me to see them go. I had begun to imagine they could live with us forever, get odd jobs in Mount Vernon as carpenters or music teachers, coach soccer, or become volunteer firemen. But the heavy metal fans of Vancouver, British Columbia, were waiting. Mötley Crüe had other cities to rock, other fuckies to group. I mean, whatever, you know what I mean. Tired, I walked back to the house to sacrifice a cat to the dark lord of the underworld.

Ryan Boudinot

On "An Essay and a Story about Mötley Crüe"

Knowing One's Audience and
Making Your Dreams Come True

This is an essay about a story about "An Essay and a Story about Mötley Crüe." Some time after I wrote whatever it is you want to call it, I read it twice in front of people at Richard Hugo House in Seattle. The first time was for an event called Cheap Wine and Poetry. The audience was tanked and I had to stop reading several times to let the laughter die down. Best reading ever. Thinking I'd get a similar reaction, I read it again to a youth writing group, many of whom were born after Mötley Crüe's heyday. Crickets. I felt old up there at the lectern, explaining that in the olden days musicians wore codpieces and urged young midwestern boys to kill their siblings by painstakingly recording messages backward in LP vinyl. Worst reading ever. But in the audience that day was a cool guy named Joe Slaby, the facilities manager for Hugo House. In a previous life Joe had worked as a roadie and drum tech for bands like Jane's Addiction and Tool. After I left the stage in shame, Joe approached me to compliment my story and mention that he *just happened* to be friends with Mötley Crüe's tour manager and that the band *just happened* to be coming through town in a few days. Would I be interested in tickets and backstage passes?

A few days later I'm at the White River Amphitheater in South King County, where Indie Rock fears to tread, and Mötley Crüe is taking the stage for their "Crüefest" reunionish tour. They brought out the pyro, the Jumbotrons, the vaguely satanic props. Man, did their music ever suck. Vince Neil, Nikki Sixx, and Mick Marrs did that heavy metal thing where they all line up next to each other with their instrument/mic stand pointed toward the crowd and rhythmically lunge together. During one song the Jumbotrons interspersed images of Donald Rumsfeld with softcore lesbian sex scenes. (My friend turned to me and said, "Since when did Noam Chomsky join the band?") Tommy Lee brought out what he called the "titty cam," inviting females to flash him so that their mammaries could be projected on the screens. I felt a twinge of anxiety as he initiated this bit, imagining the band's embarrassment in the event no female Crüe fans took him up on the offer. This was after all a postfeminist era, in which young women had been raised with a greater awareness of—oh, okay, here come the tits.

Women of South King County, forgive me my lack of faith.

After the show, my friends and I made our way to the backstage area and flashed our magical passes. Upon being ushered into the inner sanctum, we were informed that the band had swiftly departed the venue, hopping on the tour bus back to the hotel. There would be no meet-and-greet for us. As a consolation, we got to hang out in Nikki Sixx's dressing room while the inhumanly industrious road crew dismantled the set and started packing various things in crates. We stayed for about an hour, chatting with the band's backup dancer, perusing Mr. Sixx's toiletries (Arm & Hammer baking soda toothpaste), and eating from his fruit basket. I even tried on one of his belts. Didn't have the balls to try on his chaps. Word was that Mr. Sixx "read books," so I left behind a copy of the essay/story tucked into my first book, to be packed away along with the bassist's myriad scarves, scented candles, and smoking cessation medications.

Thanks, "An Essay and a Story about Mötley Crüe," for making my dreams come true!!!

Ashley Butler

Dazzle

In 1893 American engineer Simon Lake designed an omniscope for his *Protector*. Relying on eight prisms, his invention allowed the submariner a 360-degree view of the surface. But while the scope provided an upright image of the view off the bow, views off port and starboard appeared sideways, and the rear image remained inverted. Lake turned down the U.S. Navy's request to purchase his scope, claiming it came with the submarine. Six years later the Electric Boat Company developed a periscope that rotated, but as it rotated so did the image it presented. The navy continued to search for an adequate device that could also be retracted to reduce drag and minimize the visual effect of the scope on the surface as the submersible pulled through the water below. During the First World War the navy adopted the periscope designed by Sir Howard Grubb, a British telescope maker responsible for building refractors for the Vienna Observatory, Melbourne Observatory, Armagh Observatory, Coats Observatory, Paisley, and the Royal Observatory, Greenwich.

Early antisubmarine warfare focused on the site of surveillance above water: the periscope. While concealment involves hiding an object from sight, deception seeks to divert another's gaze. Although both are forms of camouflage, the goals of each approach are at odds. Whereas the concealed object may be passed over by the eye, the disrupted ship is seen but misidentified. Shadows, highlights, contour and structure, smoke from a ship's funnels, the angle of its surfaces in relation to the sun or moon as it moves across the sky, light reflecting off the waves, then hull. All of these relationships, which derive from a ship's placement within a particular environment, attract attention. The Roman army masked their fleet by dyeing the sails of their skiffs Venetian blue, which resembled the color of the sea. Their sailors wore blue uniforms to blend with their boats. In the First World War, to trouble the accurate perception of their ships, many countries asked artists to develop patterns, which were painted on the sides of warships and occasionally on merchant ships. Camoufleurs hoped their designs might distort the perception of a ship's course or speed or cause the ship to appear as two ships or no ship. They called it dazzle.

Pattern disruption relies on a tendency to determine the detail of a body from its outline. When effective, the disrupted figure appears as a collection of unrelated aspects from which the eye can resolve no certain perspective. The concept behind pattern disruption derived from artist Abbott Thayer's law of counter-shading. In "The Law That Underlies Protective Coloration," an article that would eventually secure his reputation as the father of modern camouflage, Thayer explains the principle of *counter-shading*: an animal's coat is typically darker in those areas where the sun lands, brighter where it does not, and this was due, in part, to evolutionary development. It would seem to explain why animals like pronghorns have light bellies and dark backs. By evenly distributing the amount of light across a body, Thayer claims, the animal appears two-dimensional and is only seen when seen apart from its natural environment, or by one for whom it is not prey. "The protectively colored animal is *obliterated* by his counter-gradation of shades, and in the cases where he escapes notice, it is by virtue of the eye's failure to recognize it as a solid object of any kind, seeming, if it rests on it at all, to see *through it to what is beyond*."

If vision represents a body's ability to locate itself in the world, then to destroy the submersible one destroyed the extension of its unseen shape: its sight. While the U.S. and Royal Navies developed different patterns, or measures, of camouflage to disrupt the enemy's perception of surface ships, each country's understanding of these principles of deception at sea developed in relation to a common threat. The *Unterseeboot*, or U-boat, was a German submarine employed in the First and Second World Wars, and its attacks on merchant ships, beginning in October 1914 with the sinking of the SS *Giltra*, are often cited—along with the sinking of the RMS *Lusitania* in May 1915—as a catalyst for U.S. involvement in the First World War. On September 5, 1914, the first torpedo fired by a submarine in wartime sank the British light cruiser HMS *Pathfinder*. Later that month another U-boat sank three cruisers off the Hook of Holland. Of the sight, the first watch officer on board the SM U-9 later wrote, "In the periscope, a horrifying scene. . . . We in the conning tower tried to suppress the impression of drowning men in the wreckage." By August 1915 U-boats were sinking British ships faster than they could be built.

The submarine became an origin with which people could identify their grief over catastrophic events that occurred far from witness. And the periscope was a sign of the vessel's conceit. The idea of the undersea environment as a mass grave or metaphor for death was reinforced in the British and American public conscience with the sinking of the passenger steamship RMS *Titanic* in 1912 and the sinking of the RMS *Lusitania*. In 1915 Britain established the Bureau of Invention and Research to gather and develop new ways in which to deal with the submarine threat. They welcomed ideas from officers as well as the public. It was thought that twenty-four searchlights might train light on a particularly bright moon to mitigate its luminous feature of a ship. Or that green paint dispersed across the water might coat a scope's lens as it rose, causing the officer to believe he occupied a depth not yet calculated. Another suggestion led swimmers to patrol the sea in a motorboat. When a periscope was spotted, two men would swim to the scope: one would cover it with a black hood while the other used a hammer to crack its lens. One admiral proposed training seagulls and sea lions to locate submarines by first introducing the animals to decoy scopes, out of which breadcrumbs projected with the aid of a revolving knife and pusher. Although the birds learned to flock to the device, ultimately they could not differentiate between enemy scopes and their own.

We have a tendency to first recognize the entirety of a form in the world and only then attribute losses to account for what is actually seen. It allows us to respond quickly to a threat, given minimal information. But it also forces us to make assumptions about what is meaningful with regard to our own survival and, to some extent, disregard the rest. When threatened, we require these illusions be processed as information pertaining to the perceived world; we must, in other words, believe we see the world as it is. By painting the sides of ships in the First World War it seems as if the camoufleur was attempting to merge the body with its trace—to force another to believe he sees without seeing the cause of what is seen.

Ashley Butler

On "Dazzle"

The Fluidity of Boundaries

Sight is closely tied to memory. What we see is influenced by our needs and desires and by the expectations of the larger community in which we find ourselves at a given point in time. Although we may think of history as a narrative that helps guide our actions, it may also be considered as an artifice that provides little certainty. As writers, we are constantly asking ourselves how we know what we think we know.

When I first started reading about dazzle camouflage, I thought the idea seemed both absurd and interesting. What allowed sailors to believe that ships could blend with the sea or sky to the point they would become unrecognizable to the enemy? Under what circumstances might a country believe they could alter the perception, or beliefs, of another? The credibility of the practice may have been bolstered at the time by similar ideas in Gestalt psychology and in cubism. In one famous anecdote, Picasso reportedly walked down Boulevard Raspail during World War I and said of the dazzle-painted cannon coming toward him: "C'est nous qui avons fait ça." *We have created that.* He understood that the success of an illusion, or a particular perception, relies on the beholder.

American artist Abbot Thayer came to a similar conclusion, though under far different circumstances. Following his wife's death in 1891, Thayer made dazzle his cause. He took photographs, painted, published articles, and performed demonstrations to illustrate how pattern disruption worked. I interpreted his newfound obsession as an expression of grief, his attempt to claim a sense of certainty by elucidating what was once considered unknown. It was as if he might convince himself that his experience of grief could reveal some truth about the world.

Readers and writers redraw boundaries as well, often in an effort to bolster some sense of a shared recognition at the genre's core. But truth is not consensus. Those who demand static and unchanging parameters are, perhaps, doing a disservice to the genre. In *The Republic*, Plato expresses the desire to ban poets from his city because they do not always abide by the kind of reasoning he favors. Poets challenge these boundaries of rationality by drawing on, for example, metaphor, association, image—none of which sat well with the philosopher.

We writers remain fascinated by our inability to settle on a single understanding of truth (or *nonfiction*, for that matter). Perhaps the best we can do is to practice being open to the world, to create a space so something can pass through.

Steven Church

Thirty Minutes to the End

An Essay to My Aunt Judy on the Occasion
of the May 4, 2007, Tornado

Greensburg, Kansas | May 4, 2007

9:15 p.m. | Thirty Minutes

Aunt Judy, your first question might have been: What did the man on
the radio say? Did he say tornado "emergency"? You're not even sure
what that means. Perhaps the radios vibrated with the dial-tone hum
of warning. The TV too, its signal coming in at a slightly higher pitch,
noise warbling between devices, coupled with the splash of Doppler
green, orange, and red covering your town, maybe the whole corner
of the state. This noise, this awful whine becomes an abomination, no
help at all. So you simply switch it off.

Earlier, just before dusk, you may have sat on your sunporch, newly
wallpapered, and watched the grove of trees bend and twist in the wind.
As a beginning image, I like to put you there, the last afternoon light
brushing your cheek. One last moment of quiet in this house of stories.

Outside now the noise continues. New noise. Yellow warning sirens crank up and wail around their poles. Through the small kitchen
window above your sink, the sky turns green and then bruise-colored
purple. Clouds stampede, rolling and tumbling, reaching tendrils

down, but you can barely see them in these penumbral hours of the day just before the dark of night truly falls. Now perhaps you smell the air tinged with ozone. The crackle of static. And the man on the radio tells you it is coming; not the train that blew past on the tracks; not the morning; not salvation; not the friends from church who come over sometimes in the evenings. Not yet. Not tonight. Now it is something much worse—but you cannot know these things yet, have not seen the pictures I've seen splashed in the days after. You cannot picture the sticks, the rubble, the piles of bricks, the abstract painting of scree as seen from a satellite.

9:20 p.m. | Twenty-five Minutes

You have begun to think about whether you should take this seriously. The man on the radio says ten minutes. You have ten minutes to take cover. But you've heard these warnings before. Ten minutes to the apocalypse. Twenty days to the end of the world. But just a minute ago, you stood out in the front yard, staring up at the sky with your neighbors, just like you always do when the sky really starts to churn, when a big storm is brewing. You could feel the wind on your face, tugging at your cheeks, loosening the curls in your hair, pressing the fabric of your skirt flat against your thighs. Now you are standing in the front hall of your house, the weight of your body settled into your feet. Shoes off, toes wiggling on the rug. Your big empty house haunted with ghosts of all of us. The silent piano. My brother and me peer out from walls. All the cousins. The siblings. The babies. Family Christmases. My grandparents, your parents. The holiday "shows" in this house. Your husband, Bill, sitting on a saddle mounted on a piano bench singing "I've Been So Lonely in My Saddle Since My Horse Died" and playing a tiny toy guitar.

He's gone now. Your children have moved away. Everyone gone from this place, this house, this town, this state. But the memories still dance around these rooms like mortar dust blown from the joints and seams. Motes of us, captured in the waning light, drift through stray yellow beams, still lingering in the house. Here is another image: children's voices call out from the room upstairs, the one with the electric trains, their noise rising over the tinny chug-chug and whistle of the locomotives as the walls crumble to dust around them. But that couldn't be happening yet, could it? Not now. Not yet. You still have ten minutes. There are no children left in this house. That much is true.

9:25 p.m. | Twenty Minutes

Now you have retreated to the basement, locked the door at the top of the stairs. Now you have the television on, the news reports talking to you. Telling you things. F5 they say. A massive tornado. Over a mile wide. And you think that this cannot be right, that this is too big. An exaggeration, an aberration. Nothing serious, right? A mistake. Nothing so different from other big storms on the High Plains of Kansas. But it is dark outside and you see nothing. Now you stand in the shag-carpeted TV room and wait for it. Now you know that it is real, the sirens are wailing on their poles for a reason. This season. This time. It's when the sirens stop wailing, their noise winding down, dying, that you know you're in trouble. The power cuts out. Now you cannot sit still, cannot stop pacing, rocking in the green chair, drumming your fingers on your knee and then knitting them together, tugging on your thumb. Now you are talking to God. Now you are praying, down on your knees praying. Because you can feel the wind and the rain and the dust pushing against your foundation and you know that the end is coming.

9:30 p.m. | Fifteen Minutes

Now the tornado has begun to churn through the south side of town, moving slow, sucking up cars, tossing trees, splintering homes. But you cannot see this, cannot know that some cars would be found miles away from home. Now the lights go out, the power down. Now you are truly afraid. Now you can hear it coming. Like a freight train. That's what they say. But it is much, much worse. Freight trains pass by your house all the time and they sound nothing like this. Now you will look at your son Aaron's wheelchair, built by your husband, Bill. Yellow, bright, with green script. His name. His chair. Decorated with flowers. He died too soon. All in the family. Three cousins gone, another child this past year. Both grandparents. Now you see the pictures of your family on the walls. Now perhaps you will even see that picture of my brother and my father, my mother, my stepmother, my half-brother, my son, me. Your own children. Indiana, Kansas, Chile. Now perhaps you will think those things that people think when they think that it is over. The pictures flickering past your eyes. Minutes, seconds, scenes — the stories of your life in this place rattling through the projector.

9:35 p.m. | Ten Minutes

Your parents' home must already be gone, the one south and east of you, near the high school. *God, the high school.* Crumbled. Blown to bits. This place, this building where you sang and swooned for your husband, Bill. You cannot know how the next day all that's left standing of the school where you and your children attended will be the doorway, a precarious wall of brick above it, and the stone-carved letters Greensburg High School. You cannot yet see what I see. This photograph, the glass doors untouched. An image and a metaphor. Something sublime in the scene of destruction. Two blocks away, your family's little ranch-style with its additions and expansions, growing chambers like a mollusk. But now the shell must be gone. Now you cannot know. You cannot know the way the wind blows the windows out first, pictures off their hangers, moves furniture around almost gently, nudging things around a bit. Then it picks up a wooden chair and throws it through a wall. And you've done nothing to deserve it. You too can imagine the new owners of that old house huddled in the basement, the stairs covered and locked like they do—the secret basement beneath the floor. You can imagine how they survive down there and the anguished sound of the mirrored wall and glass shelves in the living room cracking, shattering and flying like missiles into the furniture, the walls. But you cannot yet understand the way the tornado touches some things and not others, destroys everything but one wall, one photograph, one entire home untouched. You cannot yet understand how the tornado will blow out the windows and take your one box of sentimental trinkets with it. But you will. You will see. We all will see soon enough.

9:40 p.m. | Five Minutes

Now. This is it . . . . wish . . . for something. Ting. Creak. This is when it hits. Smacks your house. And the pop-pop. You have to stop thinking. Blink, shake the dust out of your hair. Wish, wish you knew who in the roar . . . who to call to reach to scream above the noise. Noise not like a train. Like a train wreck in the dark. Glass breaking. Chink-chinking. Now how the wind howls. Now the house is groaning. And you are curled up with your head tucked between your knees, your hands clasped behind your head. Wish for the end. You are waiting.

Spinning. Drifting off. The furniture scrapes on the floors upstairs, slams into the walls. The piano's cabinet resonates blows from flying debris. Certainly parts of the house are gone now. Certainly things will never be the same. The house rattles and screams, shakes like a dollhouse. Now you understand. Now you begin to think that God has done this. Now you tell yourself that this is all part of His plan. The plan. The grand plan. Because it is easier to believe that this sort of random violence happens for a reason, a purpose, a punishment. But you and I both know that there is no reason in weather. No rhyme, no order, no morality. But you are in no position now to appreciate the absurdity of the TV meteorologist, that false prophet. Right now you long for his voice, his reassuring confidence, his perfectly coifed hair. You want his voice to say, "It's over." Any voice besides the howl of this storm. Perhaps my voice? What if? What if I had decided to call you, my aunt, out of the blue? Something I never do. Ever. There are no lines of communication between us, no letters or words. What if we had been on the phone and I had heard the sirens wailing in the background, the pinched fear in your voice? What if things were different? What if you had been able to travel all the way to California through the phone lines? Maybe I could have saved you, sheltered your house from the wind.

9:45 p.m. | Zero Minutes

It is almost over now . . . . . . and there is profound quiet in the sudden absence of violence. Much greater than the calm before is the calm after, the comedown, the drop. The drain. This is when you wait in the dark for some sign. Anything. A light, a voice. The crackle of static and the radio man's voice. The whisper of the leaving wind as it races out beyond your house on the edge of town, rises up, scatters and dissipates.

The funnel loses fuel, sucks back up. But you are still down below, in the basement with the plastic toy oven and the dress-up clothes, the antique trucks and rag dolls and maybe on a shelf somewhere a cowboy-boot box that the child-me converted to an old-fashioned telephone with some tape and string. Maybe you can hear me better through this dusty box-phone, my voice wavering through the string and echoing in the cardboard. I am here. Beneath the stairs. Follow me. Find your way up. And you will rise from the basement into your kitchen. In the half-light it seems like the kitchen you knew before, everything mostly intact. It's only when your eyes adjust to the dark that you peer out into the dining room, look up, see the churning black sky. Only when you climb the stairs to rooms that no longer exist. The top two floors of your giant home cleaved, torn with the roof and tossed. This is when you know. This is when you understand. As you leave your battered home and wander out into the night, nothing looks the same. Everything gone. The streets filled with the pieces of your neighbor's homes, cars, furniture, sheets of metal. Others wander around too, crowds of people emerging from their basements. Stricken and pale. You hear crying or moaning coming from somewhere. You make your way to the Kansas Inn, the restaurant attached to the motel on the east side of town, that motel where your dad, my granddad, ate biscuits and gravy every Saturday morning. It is one of only two motels in this town. Yet you don't know anyone there. No familiar faces. Just the faces of survivors; and their grief is too public, their pain too shared. Now you are truly alone. Now you are beyond the reach of my voice. Nothing can pull you back now.

9:45 p.m. | The End

This is how it goes. A man in a truck finds you. Wandering east along Highway 54. Away from town. He has driven to Greensburg to search for his own parents. He picks you up, perhaps because you look like his mother for a split second, perhaps because you just look lost, perhaps because he knows you. He picks you up because that's all he can do. You are disoriented. Dazed. Wandering in disbelief. You cannot understand why all these people are part of your bad dream. You cannot know how the TV cameras tomorrow will pause on your house, an American flag planted in front, and they will say that the "schools were destroyed," suggesting that your house was a school. But it is just large. The schools are gone. Your house, even in ruins, towers over the flat scree around it. You cannot know how I will see this picture, that flag planted, and it will conjure up postapocalyptic images of the Statue of Liberty toppled and half-buried, a forgotten husk of copper—another iconic structure reduced to ruin. I will see your house and all the memories, every brick a story, and I will think that some part of our world has ended. Grandparents gone. The old and the young dying. My father, your brother, believes in fate. He believes that the past is the past. But he cannot know how this day, these minutes will resonate. You cannot know that a woman from Greensburg once grabbed his arm at a funeral and told him she thought our family had been cursed, or that when I think of this scene I imagine a haggard old witch in tattered clothes, a wart protruding from her chin, and one bulging all-seeing eyeball—a kind of absurd, comical image designed to temper the truth of what she says. Perhaps we are cursed. Or perhaps we create our personal apocalypses, crafted in thine own image and imagination. You cannot know how I will imagine all of this tornado, this apocalypse, this story—every detail, every image of you—as a way to stretch my voice out and let it rise and quiver from the severed lines, hovering nearby as something familiar and safe here at the end.

Steven Church

On "Thirty Minutes to the End: An Essay to My Aunt Judy on the Occasion of the May 4, 2007, Tornado"

Rethinking Genre

When it comes down to defining our discipline, nonfiction writers love to test-drive terms, looking for the ones that give us the most freedom and respect and avoid the problematic provincialism (often fundamentalism) of traditional genre classifications. Nonfiction has for a long time been the genre defined by what it is not, an aesthetic identity that conscripts many of us practitioners into a shared job of definition and, by default, into a kind of defensive position. What is it exactly that we do? What are the rules, the boundaries of the genre? Why do you think your life is interesting? More and more these days nonfiction writers are rejecting such questions, and we're rejecting terms and definitions altogether. Many of us cringe at mere mention of *memoirist*. Some of us balk at being called *creative nonfiction* writers and prefer the term *literary nonfiction*. Some of us don't even want to be known as nonfiction writers and instead prefer the term and identity *essayist*. The essayist in this understanding is a writer who employs techniques from all the other so-called genres in a mode of exploring consciousness . . . or something like that.

   This idea of essaying as a mode of thought and writing isn't new, but it is a kind of rejection of the traditional, rigid understanding of genre as fiction, nonfiction, or poetry (and even of the further classification into subgenres). And as much as I like this move and the freedom it grants me as a writer, I'm not sure it really saves us from the provincialism of genre classification, from the seemingly insatiable drive to categorize and moralize, or from the "minimum security prison" that David Shields calls genre in his book *Reality Hunger*. So what if we do away with terms like *fiction*, *nonfiction*, *poetry*, *drama*, and just talk about *modes* of writing and thinking? Where does it leave us?

If I say, for instance, that I don't believe genre matters and that what I'm mostly interested in is essaying as a mode of thinking on the page (true), does that move us forward in our understanding of what exactly nonfiction is? I'm interested in exploration and digression. But does this escape the breakdown into subgenres or sub-modes? Probably not. We still are left then trying to understand the difference between, for example, "lyrical," "journalistic," or "imaginative" modes of essaying, still encamping ourselves in one mode versus another, still just trading the term *genre* for another. We're still conscripted into the shared project of definition.

Much of the time you can probably put me in the "imaginative" or even "lyrical" camps of essaying, modes of writing that (at least in my mind) necessarily blur the boundaries between genres but that are also long-established modes of writing. But I did not set out to write a genre-bending piece with "Thirty Minutes to the End." I just wanted to write something in response to the destruction of my father's hometown. The subject chose its own form and style and I mostly just jumped aboard for the ride.

On May 4, 2007, an F5 tornado nearly a mile wide with winds over 280 mph plowed through my father's hometown of Greensburg, Kansas, destroying 95 percent of the structures and killing eleven people. Aunt Judy, the only family member left there, waited out the storm in the basement of her home. The next day I stared at satellite photos of the aftermath and couldn't believe the reality of the devastation, could barely even recognize the place. I'd spent many weeks during the summer, holidays, and other times in the tiny farm community of Greensburg. My brother and I lost ourselves exploring my aunt's stately old home at the edge of town, right next to the railroad tracks, where we learned all the nooks and crannies, all the hidden places. Young writers are always told to write what they know, and I knew both the physical and emotional landscape pretty well.

Before I wrote this essay, though, I never talked with Aunt Judy about the tornado, never interviewed her or asked her to tell me about her experience. I have no eyewitness accounts, no notes or photographs. I did little actual research. Though the decision wasn't perhaps conscious at the time I wrote the essay, I did reject more "journalistic" modes of writing in favor of trusting my imagination. I believe my dad e-mailed me a sparse summary of what had happened to my aunt during and after the storm, but this was the only text I had to use besides national news stories in various publications, most of which I read quickly, cataloging important details. Though I'm from Kansas, I've never lived through a tornado and have no real understanding of what it might be like. If you read the essay and think otherwise, then I suppose you could call what I'm doing a kind of lying.

In the essay I use my imagination, employing techniques of fiction — specifically the re-creation of the *reality* of the experience — as a way to essay themes of memory and family, as well as ideas of connection and disconnection, community, loss, and landscape. I wanted the piece to reflect the idea of an essay as a kind of offering, a reaching out to my aunt and to the audience, as well as my own effort to explore the meaning of this event. I wanted it to sound a little bit like a letter — granted, a letter that reaches for something more — and I also wanted the second-person address to create a tension between the immediacy of the detail and the distancing of the point of view, with the first-person I showing up only briefly in the beginning and again at the end, hopefully showing my distance from the events but also my intimacy with both my aunt and the place.

I wrote the whole piece in a couple of days, or at least the first draft of it, focusing on detail and time management, inventing, adding, and embellishing wherever I needed to in order to keep the immediacy and movement in the essay. To me, despite the overt fictionalizing—creation of setting, character, present action, and so on—the fabrication of details, and the re-creation of events I never witnessed, even secondhand, this piece has always been a rather personal essay. It has always been nonfiction. It is then perhaps a piece that reflects well my own beliefs about the boundaries of nonfiction—namely that there are none but those the writer creates for himself or that the essay chooses for itself—and hopefully a piece of writing that testifies to the importance of employing one's imagination as a mode of essaying.

Stuart Dybek

Bait

Despite the shadowy shaft of light, clouded even on the brightest days, visibility was good. You could peer fathoms down to a bottom where the contours of broken flowerpots and fogged bottles took shape amidst a cobble of trash. Spongy knobs of moss bordered the foundation, and in the corners you could see silty webs, but not their spiders. The screwdriver that had plunged four stories was visible, too, its luminescent yellow handle resting beside what appeared to be the rotted arm of a doll. My father who could fix most anything had been using it to pry my bedroom window higher so that the room would be less stuffy on the hot summer nights. The window opened on what we referred to as an airshaft, although the so-called air smelled like an updraft of must. Leaning out for better leverage in a way that made me worry he'd fall, my father had lost the grip on the screwdriver when he'd banged his funny bone on the window frame.

"Da damn, sonny boy," he said, mournfully rubbing his elbow, "that was my favorite screwdriver."

Even then, when his pliers, hammers, and wrenches still fit in the tool bag he kept in the closet atop his accordion case, years before he would buy the brick six-flat on Washtenaw and the capacity of the tool bag would be expanded by an unfinished basement that gradually filled with grinders, pipe threaders, buzz saws that threatened amputation, a torch and welder's mask, guns—pneumatic nail guns, caulking guns, mortar guns, solder guns—grouters, routers, a Roto-rooter that could reach to China, I knew how my father valued tools. I'd seen that screwdriver do everything from dismantling engines to opening sardine cans whose tabs had popped off and couldn't help but feel it had been sacrificed so that I might breathe easier.

The day after the screwdriver was lost, my father brought home from the factory a brown lunch bag embossed with greasy fingerprints from which he emptied onto my bed a chunk of metal that looked like what I imagined a meteorite might. Its surface was machined to a dull, gray-pitted luster, and its edges were rough as broken rock. It was heavy enough to make an impression on the bedspread.

My father worked on the reaper line at the Harvester factory. He'd been employed there since he'd been forced by the illness of his father to quit high school at seventeen. He'd recently been promoted to foreman. The factory was on Western Avenue, within walking distance from our house. When on weekdays at 5:00 p.m. church bells chimed and factory whistles blew, I imagined I could hear the Harvester whistle and knew that, unless he was working overtime, my father in his oily, steel-toed shoes would be taking the shortcut of Blue Island Avenue, a street that ran on an angle, on his way back home.

Once, when I was little, he'd taken me to the factory, proud to show me where he worked, and the racket of the production lines, the foundry-scorched air, and the weariness on the grimy faces of the men had frightened me and made me cry, shaming him. It was a story always told in tandem with how, on my first trip to the Riverview amusement park, when he took me into the House of Horrors, I began to scream, and he had to carry me upstream against the crowd and back out the entrance. He never failed to add that at least he got them to refund our tickets. I vaguely remembered both incidents and of the two, the clanging Harvester factory with its nostril-searing furnaces was the more terrifying. The metal chunk resting on my bed looked like it could have been spit out white-hot from one of those furnaces.

"Feel this, sonny boy," he said.

I weighed it in cupped hands, almost expecting it to still be throwing heat. It felt dense.

"What is it?" I asked.

"Bait," he said.

We sat on the edge of the bed while, with many twists and intricate knots, my father tied the metal bait to the end of a ball of brown twine he'd bought for a kite we'd yet to fly—a kite we'd yet to make. My father told me that when he was a kid, he and his buddies fashioned homemade kites from newspaper and sticks they trimmed with jackknives. We were going to use the funnies page from the Sunday Trib for our kite so that it flew in color.

He stood up and gave our bait a few test bobs. Satisfied that it was tied securely, he raised my bedroom window to as far as he'd managed to pry it before he'd dropped the screwdriver. We both leaned over the sill while my father paid out line from the ball of twine. The line twisted and the heavy weight at its end spun on its way down. When it finally touched bottom, my father began to jig it.

"Got it!" he said and grinned. He reeled up slowly, hand over hand, winding the twine back on the ball. I could see the screwdriver dangling by its tip.

"Reel her in, sonny boy," my father said, handing the line to me. "Don't let it bang on the side of the wall or we'll lose her."

He gripped my belt loops so I wouldn't plunge out the window. I leaned out over the airshaft and carefully wound the twine back over the ball I clutched with both hands. I could feel the pendulous weight of the bait and the screwdriver dangling at the end of our line. When there were only a few feet left to go, my father pulled me back in and reached down and hoisted up the screwdriver.

"Lucky you don't have any fillings yet cause this will yank them right out of your teeth," he said, handing me the chunk of metal. To prove his point, he dropped his key ring on the bed and when I dangled the magnet above it, the keys leapt up to attach themselves. I tugged against the powerful invisible force to free them, then took the magnet into the kitchen and started on the silverware.

In my twenties, I'd move to an island where I could fish every day; I'd buy a faded wooden boat from one of the local fishermen who jigged for kingfish with hand lines; I'd paint the boat candy-apple red and anchor where the reef dropped off into blue depths of such clarity that I could see the schools of yellowtail rising to my bait like iron filings to a magnet and the silver flash of barracuda drawn to the hooked yellowtail. The magnetism of bait made me think of the airshaft on Eighteenth Street and of my first fishing trip—with my father, as first fishing trips should be—a trip that would remain our most productive: that screwdriver was the only thing I'd ever see my father catch.

Stuart Dybek

On "Bait"

The Hybridity of Form

I wrote "Bait" to read as a stand-alone personal essay, but it's primarily a chapter from St. Stuart, an in-progress manuscript that I think of as a comic nonfiction novel. Other chapters from that same in-progress manuscript have appeared as self-contained pieces in magazines, including Harper's, BOMB!, Five Points, Playboy, ESPN Magazine, The Atlantic, and in anthologies. Some of the pieces have been published as nonfiction, others as fiction, but regardless of the genre, each chapter passes what I think of as the "No shit, you guys, this really happened" test. Friends in my neighborhood occasionally employed that phrase when we got to trading stories. If it isn't any more persuasive than a term like "reality TV," that's understandable.

The first piece I wrote for what would become St. Stuart was "Thread," a story about a boy—Stuart—who breaks the fast required on pain of mortal sin before receiving Communion by swallowing a thread. The editor who accepted it asked if it was fiction or nonfiction. I replied that genre hadn't been a consideration while I was writing it. "Thread," like "Bait," was based on something that happened to me (no shit, really, you guys), but over the years I'd published a number of like autobiographical stories as fiction. The editor said the magazine was short on nonfiction for that issue so if it was all the same to me, it would appear as nonfiction. Later Harper's republished the piece as nonfiction and it also appeared in nonfiction anthologies. Had "Thread" been published originally as fiction, it probably would not have been reprinted.

By the time I wrote "Bait," I knew it was part of a book-length project. However, I still regard having to identify it as nonfiction or fiction to be a decision from *outside* the story. The decision means more to that made-up abstraction called the reader than it does to me. In the unique, mysterious, dynamic collaboration between reader and writer, it is the imagined reader who often enforces the expectations that come with genre. If I think of "Bait" as self-contained I have no problem regarding it as an essay, but when I think of it as a chapter I feel more comfortable continuing to hedge on what it is.

When I attended the Iowa Writers' Workshop, I "studied"—a term in this instance to be taken as loosely as possible—with Frederick Exley. Fred was the author of *A Fan's Notes*, a highly praised book about a drunken rascal named Fred Exley. He called it a fictional memoir. It was published in 1968, a time when writers like Truman Capote and Norman Mailer were writing nonfiction novels, and the same year that Frank Conroy's seminal memoir *Stop-Time* appeared. It seemed then that Conroy and Exley were working along the same trajectory. Each admired the other's book. My own preference is for *Stop-Time*, but I remain fascinated by how Exley, in calling his book a fictional memoir, not only gives himself permission to locate a story on the permeable border between fiction and nonfiction but calls the reader's attention to it.

Conroy's memoir depends on the intimate, credible relationship it establishes with the reader. It's not to Conroy's advantage to raise the issue of fact or fiction. Exley's book, despite tragic elements, inclines toward the comic, and comedy often requires exaggeration. For me, the term *fictional memoir* signals that the writer's allegiance is divided between remembered "fact" and invention. Even if discussing his book with Fred over drinks—long conversations, many drinks—hadn't confirmed the liberties he'd taken with the conventional memoir form, it would be clear to me as a reader that in *A Fan's Notes* the creation of comic episodes trumps the allegiance to memory.

In describing "Bait" as a chapter in a comic nonfiction novel, I'm trying to indicate that allegiance to comedy—not necessarily to ha-ha funny, but to the comic in the broadest sense of the term. That allegiance asserts itself at conception, as the elements selected out of memory are those that will lend themselves to a comic treatment. Memoir, which depends on trust between reader and writer, comes with the handy built-in caveat that memory, while objectively unreliable, is subjectively true. Rather than choose the blank page of forgetting, it is the nature of the memoirist to research or to invent. Take dialogue, for instance—unless the memoirist is relying on scrupulously kept journals, how can remembered dialogue help but be invented? Oddly, for the reader, the loophole that memory is unreliable confers credibility on the genre rather than distrust. So if invention is tacitly allowed—that is, unless you get caught by Oprah—then why bother with a term such as *fictional memoir*?

Terms such as *fictional memoir* and *nonfiction novel* are hybrids in the way that memoir is not. They invite the reader to participate in the interplay of fact and fiction. Hybrid terms for hybrid genres are common enough to modernism and postmodernism. The prose poem, the lyrical essay, the novel in stories, and the nonfiction novel are all hybrids that imply not just contradiction, but paradox. Paradox for me is a method by which a writer explores mystery, and I've been drawn to each of those genres.

Beth Ann Fennelly

Salvos into the World of Hummers

It hatches from an egg the size of a Le Sueur English pea, weighing one-fiftieth of an ounce. Even fully grown, they're so light that you could send eight of them for the price of a first-class stamp.

But the fact that they are small and beautiful (Audubon called them "glittering garments of the rainbow") is not the only reason why I like hummingbirds. No, for that gets them dismissed as precious. Who else likes hummingbirds? There are two groups. The first is composed of sweet old ladies who crochet antimacassars. (I am anti antimacassars.) This group likes the idea of the hummingbird. The second group is composed of grizzled men in their sixties and seventies who drive huge rusted pickups and stalk the birds and log their statistics the way their neighbors might study draft picks. This second group loves hummers because they understand who hummers are. Which is this: engineering marvels. And shit-kicking badasses.

These men are almost as driven as the hummers they study: Fred Bassett, former air force pilot ("Following flying things is second nature to me"). James Bell, master bander in three states, a computer specialist for Shell Oil. Bob Sargent, electrician, and cofounder with his wife, Martha, of the Hummer/Bird Study Group. Their house in Clay, Alabama, is the original H BSG station and over thirty thousand ruby throats have been banded there. Bob is famous with hummingbird enthusiasts for, among other things, banding the same ruby throat eight years in a row. Because relatively little is known about hummingbirds, nearly all data collected add to the sum of what is known, and these three men have collected a lot of it (according to the H BSG pamphlet,

"HBSG affiliated banders hold nearly 25% of the banding permits issued by the Bird Banding Laboratory"). Sargent's eight-year banded bird flies in the face of (excuse the pun) previous beliefs that the ruby throat life cycle was around four years. Also, until recently, it was believed that ruby throats were the only hummers found east of the Mississippi. But the HBSG's recent data refute this; members have banded in that region "thirteen other species: Rufous, Allen's, Broad-tailed, Buff-bellied, Calliope, Black-chinned, Magnificent, Anna's, Costa's, Green Violet-ear, White-eared, Broad-billed, and Green-breasted Mango."

An eager mixologist, twice a week I make my hummer cocktail, four parts water to one part sugar, boil it and stir it and cool it and fill the nectar well. Yes, they eat sugar, but that does not make them sweet.

I like them because—I'm not supposed to write this, much less think it, for I will be accused of anthropomorphism—they like me. I like them because they have become my pets. Or I have become theirs.

They are much more than merely small (though the bee hummingbird is the smallest bird on earth, and I've seen a photo of one perched quite commodiously on a pencil eraser). And they are much more than merely beautiful (though they are that; the first Spanish explorers called them *joyas voladoras*, flying jewels—in fact, they're compared to jewels so often that hummingbird aviaries in zoos throughout the world are known as "jewel rooms").

They are also unique in startling ways. They're fast—they have the most rapid wingbeat of all birds, reportedly up to two hundred per second, and reliably to eighty per second. Their flight muscles make up 30 percent of their weight. They can fly up to sixty miles per hour during courtship dives and juice one thousand flowers a day (so many flowers, in fact, that one way experts determine the age of hummers is by examining the bill, to see if the grooves have been worn down by friction). And they're smart—percentage-wise, they have the largest brains of all birds, 4.2 percent. And they're hugely kinetic—they have the greatest relative energy output of any warm-blooded animal. The ratio of their heart size to their body size is the largest of all warm-blooded animals, and their heartbeat reaches 1,260 beats per second. And they're dexterous—they're the only birds that can rotate their wings in a circle, so they're the only ones that can fly forward, backward, up, down, sideways, hover, and even, for short distances, fly upside down. (The logo of the American Helicopter Society is the hummingbird.) And lastly, they're efficient. Although they eat up to eight times their weight daily and have a metabolism one hundred times an elephant's, they alone among birds can enter the trancelike state called torpor, come evening, in which they perch on a branch and fluff up their feathers, slowing the rate of their heart and breath and lowering their temperature to conserve energy.

We're doing an addition to our house because we have a new baby on the way. The construction guys often traverse the patio where we have our feeders. Mississippi is not, for the most part, as segregated as movies would have you believe, but the teams of construction guys who've worked in waves on our house are as segregated and specific as medieval guilds. First, the Hispanic men, who took down the old wall and laid the new foundation and cursed softly in Spanish and sang softly in Spanish while they worked. Then came the team of black bricklayers, my favorite, because they seemed to enjoy themselves so much—I could hear their stories and brags over the rhythmic thunking of their trowels against the bricks: "And I said, 'Little Poot, you ain't even SEEN a lightning bolt,'" and then the huge laughter, and me on the other side of the wall laughing too though I didn't hear enough of the joke to appreciate it. Then at last the smaller team of white electricians, surly and expensive. "Can you adjust the dish while you're up there?" shouted the contractor to one electrician, balanced on the roof pitch. "Yah," answered the electrician, spitting tobacco juice down into the holly, "but it'll cost you extra."

Again, I'm probably not supposed to be noticing or commenting on these things—generalizations can sound like stereotypes—but I am pregnant and moon-dreamy and noticing. Not doing—noticing. And the hummers repay my interest. They're better than daytime drama. There's a dominant male who perches in the Bradford pear, hidden by leaves, waiting for another hummer to even think about sipping his nectar. Should one try, male or even one of the females, he zings after them and chases them away, then loops back to his perch and resettles himself with a cartoonish fluffing of his neck gorget. Four or five years ago, before I knew much about hummers, I assumed he must be worried that the nectar would run out. So I bought a second feeder and hung it in the second pear tree. But his aggressiveness was never about having enough nectar, it turns out, but protecting his turf. Now he has twice as much nectar and is twice as aggressive, chasing competition from two feeders. This little thug would wear Doc Martens if he had them, tag the branches with spray-paint.

When the first set of workers was laying the foundation, occasionally I would hear a commotion, some yelling and hooting, and if I push-heaved myself up from the couch I could see one of them running across the patio and waving his arms over his head while his coworkers laughed bright laughter. I couldn't quite figure out what tomfoolery was going on. Then came the second team of workers, and they did the same thing, but because they were talkers, I soon found out why. Apparently, they were being dive-bombed by my hummingbirds. Maybe because the men's yellow hardhats looked like flowers? The dominant male would needle down from the Bradford in large U-shaped salvos, angling directly for whoever had gotten too close, lifting up just inches from his head, then swooping down again.

"Mean little fuckers," said the crew chief, named B7, while we stood watching the hummer resettle on his branch. B7 chuckled and shook his head, and then, "Sorry for the language."

I wanted to tell him that hummers don't bite, that it would be like being attacked by a Q-tip, but he was already hitching up his tool belt and turning away. I walked inside, musing. The reason I hadn't guessed the men were being chased is that the hummers had never done anything like that to me, never once, and had never dive-bombed my husband or our children. Because they recognize me. They know the hand that feeds them and those who belong to that hand.

Bob Sargent says that hummingbirds recognize their humans, absolutely. It's become a bit of a problem for him in his work as a bander. Sometimes he bands a bird and catches it a subsequent year or two in the same place, and then they start altering their flight pattern, dodging and fainting when they see his truck. "They know your truck?" I asked. "They can see a nectar source three-quarters of a mile away," he said. "Of course they know my truck."

The best story about the hummingbird's powers of recognition comes from *The Hummingbirds of North America*, by Paul A. Johnsgard, published by Smithsonian in 1983. It tells of a scientist named Fitzpatrick who, in 1966,

placed a hummingbird feeder outside his bedroom window while he was recuperating from tuberculosis in a California sanitarium. Soon a rufous hummingbird took possession of the feeder, and thereafter Fitzpatrick watched it closely for several months. When he was finally able to go outside in a wheelchair, Fitzpatrick was immediately "greeted" by the hummingbird, which careened around his head and hovered in front of his eyes. After almost a year, when Fitzpatrick returned to his home some 13 kilometers away, the rufous somehow managed to follow him and took up residence near his house. Later, the bird usually accompanied him on his daily walks. It sometimes called his attention to the presence of other animals that he might have otherwise overlooked—once noting a half-hidden rattlesnake—and eventually rode on the rawhide lace that served as a rifle sling. When he had fully recovered from his illness, Fitzpatrick left his house for a month. Yet, only moments after he returned and got out of his car, the hummingbird was there, zooming about his head and hovering in front of his eyes!

Another reason they inspire wonder is because we know so little about them. There are no hummingbird fossils, so their evolution is largely conjectural. They've been difficult for taxonomists to classify. Six new species were discovered in the 1970s, according to Johnsgard, so more may exist. Because they are so small and fast, they're hard to study, so we still know very little about their mating habits, or why a female chooses one male over another, except that females seem to prefer the meanest, most aggressive males. We know they don't have a big songbook but what vocalizations they do make are still largely uninterpreted. (Joke told by my nine-year-old: "Why do hummingbirds hum? Because they don't know the words.")

In fact, until the 1970s people didn't quite know, or couldn't quite believe, in the hummingbirds' seasonal migration. Come early autumn, ruby throats move south from their breeding grounds, gorging on food to double their weight (to roughly two pennies' worth). Then they lift off one evening and fly through the night, a trip of five hundred miles without stopping, over the Gulf, to winter in Mexico. It was so hard for people to believe the hummingbirds were capable of this flight that the myth developed (and is still believed) that hummers would hitch rides on the backs of geese. Then, the story goes, a guy working an oil derrick in the middle of the Gulf of Mexico was suddenly surrounded by thousands of them—a huge electrical storm had forced them to land on the only surface available. And he had a camera, so he was believed. Now there are groups of hummingbird fanatics (yes, I'm one) who post their migrant sightings online, marking an interactive map so others farther north can get their feeders ready. We veteran bartenders know from experience that if you're late getting your feeder out, veteran hummers will hover in front of the window where you usually place your feeder. And they won't look happy.

Sargent and the others in the Hummer/Bird Study Group believe that some hummers, perhaps more and more due to global warming, are skipping the cross-Yucatan trek and overwintering in the southern Gulf states. With the fervency of Jehovah's Witnesses, they urge us to keep our feeders out all winter. If we spot a winter hummer (any species lingering past November 15; apparently, you can see them sometimes trying to draw nectar from red Christmas lights), we're to phone an HBSG member immediately, who will come band our bird. "We're going to have buff-bellied hummers breeding in Mississippi in a few years," predicts Fred Bassett. Bassett, now perhaps in his sixties, gives a hummer-banding demonstration every year at the Hummingbird Migration Celebration, held at the Strawberry Plains Audubon Center in Holly Springs, Mississippi. The center is housed in the 1851 Davis House, surrounded by gardens with the native plants that hummers adore. The hummers pass through on their migratory routes during September in such vast numbers that I've heard them described many times as a river, and so they seem. These fiercely independent birds that do not flock nevertheless come in such numbers that their bodies form a river of roiling iridescent emerald.

The festival includes talks and demonstrations about wildlife, endangered species, invasive species, and gardening, and there are dozens of feeders set up by the large windows where visitors can sit in rocking chairs and watch the hummers' antics. But the highlight for sure is the hummingbird banding tents. Here is where one finds Fred Bassett hard at work, surrounded by those antimacassar women who wield sharp elbows to ensure an unimpeded view. Bassett is a full-time volunteer with HBSG. If that strikes you as a sweet hobby, Bassett reveals what "full time" means: in the five months before the festival, he'd been home only ten days. The others, he'd been on the road, banding.

As Bassett lifts a bird from the mesh netting where it'd been temporarily trapped, he gathers data that is recorded by another volunteer. He measures bill length ("14.97 millimeters") and weight ("2.77 ounces") and determines gender (while the full-grown males have the easily discernible ruby throat and are one-third smaller than full-grown females, the immature males look like females and other factors must be considered, such as the females' white-tipped tail feathers). When he's recorded the data, he selects a tiny metal C-shaped band and with his pliers clamps it over the hummer's leg. The band is so small it fits over Lincoln's eye in a penny, and the relative weight, says Bassett, is "comparable to a wristwatch on a human." Each band has been photoengraved with a serial number that is filed with the Bird Banding Laboratory so if someone encounters the bird later, he or she can report it toll free to 1-800-327-BAND (and receive a certificate of appreciation). Through analyzing data, BBL learns the birds' natural history, abundance from year to year, and migration details. "A hum I banded in Alabama was found in Alaska," Bassett says with pride.

He pushes back the jeweler's magnifying eyepiece onto his forehead and holds out the banded claw to the onlookers. To show us the hummer's fat deposit, he then blows through a plastic straw onto the breast of the hummer, which separates its feathers so we can see what looks like a little blister. Then he lets several onlookers extend their palms so Bassett can rest the hummer there and they can feel the rapid heartbeat. Then he lets it go.

I have felt that heartbeat. I have felt it in my hand.

This was perhaps six years ago. I think it was the thing that started me down this spiraling flight into the world of the ruby throats. What happened was this: I was picnicking with a friend and she had to leave her house for a few moments to drive her daughter to a birthday party. So I started clearing the picnic table and moving the food to the screened-in porch. I was carrying a big bowl of ripe tomatoes and balanced it on my hip to fling open the screen door when I saw out of the far side of my eye a flash of scarlet, heard a high-pitched drone, like a small plane far away. I looked at the screen door, and it was pierced by a needle—the bill of a hummingbird, furiously winging. I watched, waiting for it to maneuver free. But it could not. It tugged its body so frantically I was afraid it would snap its bill right off. It called a harsh "tchick-tchick" that scared me. Later, I'd learn from my hummingbird listserv that usually by the time you find a hummer caught in a screen, it has died.

Had there been someone else to do it, I would have let someone else do it. But I was alone. And it was probably the bowl of tomatoes I hipped that had lured him, after all. So I set the bowl down and gently I put my nervous hand to the nervous bird, hoping it would rest easy, but it flung itself hysterically up and ricocheted back. I closed my fingers over it and stilled the wings. It was so small, small as a pinky, and terrified. I could feel its heartbeat fluttering in the hollow of my hand, and felt my own faster than normal. I twisted it clockwise. I unscrewed that bird. Then I held my palm flat and waited for it to zip away. It rested there—perhaps too stunned to move at first, I don't know, but it seemed like a moment of grace, of hummer gratitude, one-Mississippi, two-Mississippi, three-Mississippi; then the lightning. Good-bye, good-bye.

Consider that a hummer has a brain the size of a BB. Then, think of the information packed inside. Do you remember every good restaurant where you've eaten? Hummers do, and they stop at the same food-rich sites each year on their migrations. It appears that this is actually hard-wired into their genetic codes, because even hatchling-year hummers feed at traditional sites. They've inherited knowledge of these locations from their ancestors.

So, too, do the hummers like to build a nest in the exact spot where they were born. Hummingbirds have fidelity. So, starting in February, the ruby throats leave their wintering grounds (some as far south as Panama) and begin to move north, doubling their weight again to a pudgy two ounces. The males move first. They top off their tanks near dusk one evening in the Yucatan and then lift into the air, flying nonstop for the next eighteen to twenty-two hours until they make landfall somewhere along the Gulf. Hummers don't all fly the same night but have staggered starts spread out over a few weeks, which ensure that, should bad weather occur, the entire population won't be wiped out. When they hit land, they refuel, then continue to migrate north, to their ancestral birthplace, some to the same tree, even the same branch. I tested this information one year by tying a twisty-tie to the branch where my male hummer guarded the feeder, and it's true, he chose the same perch the following year. (I like to watch hummers land. Their bodies curve into a C-shape, wings lifted, tail tucked. There should be a yoga pose called Hummingbird.)

The female follows the migrating male perhaps ten days later. By now the male has already established his breeding territory, which he fiercely defends, flying each morning to the corners of his site to utter his harsh call, the aural equivalent of a dog's urine markings. These returning males are horny as hell and brilliantly colored, having just completed a full molt. (They remind me of our human snowbirds who come back from southern climes with loud shirts and tans.) The males won't look so spiffy again. Their appearance declines as they spend all their time defending their territory from other males. Usually a harsh scolding will do, especially if accompanied by a bit of posturing, the puffing out of the red gorget to appear bigger. But the defending hummer will fight if he needs to, body-slamming his opponent or grasping wing feathers in his bill to yank them out. Once the challenger is chased away, the male returns, king of the roost, and crows about it. If he loses, there's a new king.

When the females arrive, the male settles down a bit, and eventually he might allow a female to feed in his territory; then he follows her as she flies away. In neutral territory they'll complete mating dives, large U-shaped swoops. If she's receptive, they'll mate, which takes about two seconds. And that's the extent of the hummer marriage. She'll build the nest and raise the hatchlings herself.

Unlike, say, a hen, who builds a nest and then lays eggs in it, with both eggs and nest remaining the same size throughout, the hummer mama builds a nest that grows for eggs that grow. And me, with my stretching skin, my belly expanding to hold my expanding son, six pounds now says the ultrasound technician, how could I not admire the hummingbird mama? And here in this house with a hole, this addition predicted to be finished by fall but the drywall's not up, the windows ordered late and in the wrong size, how could I not marvel at her engineering efficiency?

This is what I've learned from *Ruby-Throated Hummingbird*, by Robert Sargent, published by Stackpole Books in 1999: "Within the brain of a female ruby-throat there lie many miracles, none more beautiful and amazing than the blueprint for her nest, which includes detailed instructions for location, materials, shape, and size." She starts to build this nest before she's even found a mate. Soon, two eggs will be ripening within her. Sometimes a female is able to repair her nest from the previous year, but if the nest is in dire straits she'll build from scratch in the same area. New construction takes six to eight days. (Wise and wily hummer, I think, as our construction project stretches from six months to eight.) Much effort is made to select a branch "strong and flexible, able to withstand being severely blown about by the wind. It cannot droop lower than three yards when battered by heavy rainfall." Also, "the limb selected is almost always about pencil size" and "located near the tip of a downward-sloping branch" and covered with foliage to shade the babies, which hatch blind, black, and naked.

And of what are the nests made? The base is constructed of thistle and dandelion down and animal hairs. Sometimes I've cleaned out my brush and strung the long red hair along the dense shrubs that line our property, pleased to imagine my locks might be of use. The hummer attaches these fibers to the branch with super-strong spider web (taking any opportunity to eat any "spiders or prey ensnared in the web if she can swallow them," says Sargent). With her bill, she'll apply tree sap as glue. Sargent notes, "All during the nest building process, she periodically sits in the nest and squirms about, fitting the interior to just the right size for her body."

After this base is constructed, she builds the sidewall, thickest near the base and attenuating as it rises so "the rim of the nest will stretch like fine elastic material," eventually flattening out to accommodate the growing hatchlings until the nest resembles a launching pad, which, of course, is what it will become. The nest when completed is about 1.5 inches tall, the circumference of a quarter, "resembling half an English walnut."

It seems, with such a blueprint, that nests should be easy to locate, but female ruby throats are master camoufleurs. They use the lichens and mosses already found on the branch, pasting these gray flakes to their nests with more sap and webs. In photos, the nest looks like a small bump, the green patina of weathered copper. Sargent notes that while she builds, the female sings little so as not to draw attention to her nest and rarely takes a direct route when flying to it.

And sometime in this process the two-second marriage occurs, her eggs are fertilized, and she'll lay one half-inch-sized egg, and then, a few days later, the second. Incubation takes perhaps two weeks. When the eggs hatch, the mother leaves the nest only to gather food, growing thinner and weaker herself during these three weeks. When she returns to the nest, the hatchlings' sensitive downy feathers are ruffled by the mother's wings, which triggers their heads to pop up and their beaks to yawp open. She then inserts her bill into the crop of her nestlings and regurgitates nectar and small bugs. If you find a nest and want to see the hatchlings' faces, you can trigger the same instinct by blowing lightly on their backs. It reminds me of how a nursing baby turns on instinct to its mother, how his mouth opens when his cheek is brushed lightly with the nipple. About three weeks after hatching, during which time the hatchlings have grown feathers and exercised their wings, they fledge. Meanwhile the mother usually builds a second nest nearby, for what is typically a two-nest cycle before migration season.

It would be handy to have a crop, a little sac in one's throat that can expand to store extra vittles. In this way, hummers remind me of another of my favorite animals, the sea otter. Sea otters have a pouch of fat in their thighs where they can store a morsel of food, a half-eaten fish, say. No wonder they roll the salty waves with such glee, thinking of snack time.

I've never seen a praying mantis kill a hummer, but I've seen one lurking on the branch above my feeder, ready to drop. I was deciding whether to remove him, evaluating the philosophical ramifications of interfering in the food chain (made more difficult by the fact that praying mantises are pretty cool, too), when the fellow got tired of waiting; he ate a wasp instead and leapt away.

My HummingbirdHobNob listserv has a thread about people finding hummingbirds in spiders' webs and releasing them. Though hummers eat spiders, too, so I'm not sure that intervention is fair. Nor am I sure what snake lovers would make of the following anecdote, recorded in *Hummingbirds of the Caribbean*, by Esther Quesada Tyrrell, Crown Publishers, 1990: "A person who had been observing the growth of two nestlings noticed a whipsnake coiled near the now-empty nest. He killed it on the spot and found the two babies inside. Incredibly, one was still alive! It was returned to its nest where it continued to thrive and eventually fledge." Historically, the hummingbird's biggest predator has been humankind. Victorian ladies in particular loved to decorate hats, shoes, and fans with the birds. A shipping record from a Brazilian port in that era shows up to three thousand hummingbird carcasses shipped per day.

I like the idea of contributing to the HBSG's quest to prove that hummingbirds are overwintering in Mississippi so, come October, I don't take my feeder in. All that month and the next, and in December when our addition is finished at last, I am there in my winter parka that no longer zips over my belly, dumping and refilling the untouched nectar. But I never do host a winter hummer. I feel oddly rejected. I laid out the banquet but the bridegroom never came.

In Brazil, they are called *beija flor*: flower kissers.

But they don't actually kiss flowers, or suck them, or use their bills as straws; they lap up nectar like a cat lapping milk from a bowl. They use their bill to protect their long, forked tongue, which when not in use is retracted and coiled into the skull. The hummingbird tongue is being studied by scientists such as MIT's John W. M. Bush, who has demonstrated that the three-quarter-inch-long tongue, once inserted into a flower, curls "into a cylinder just one twenty-fifth of an inch in diameter," according to a *New York Times* science piece published November 23, 2009. Thus the tongue forms a tube that draws nectar up because of surface tension. The hummer scrapes his tongue and swallows, repeating this process twenty times a second. Bush presented these findings at a meeting of the American Physical Society's Division of Fluid Dynamics, believing they could be useful "to researchers building miniature chemistry laboratories—so-called labs on a chip—that have to move tiny droplets of chemicals around" and could take advantage of surface tension. He reminded the scientists present, "Nature has already solved these problems."

I suppose my crush on ruby throats could have been predicted. I've always been fascinated by miniatures. I have a grain of rice on which my name has been carved in Japanese calligraphy. I spent many Alice-in-Wonderland hours as a girl wandering the Thorne Miniature Rooms at the Art Institute of Chicago, sixty-eight model rooms constructed on a scale of one inch to one foot, displaying European and American interiors, chandeliers that really illuminate, armoires hung with silken smoking jackets. I'm not alone in admiring the miniature, either; I frequent the museum here at the University of Mississippi where I teach, and despite the strong collection of southern folk art, the most requested, most viewed item is the 1930s set of costumed fleas, arranged behind a magnifying glass that you peer through to admire their embroidered outfits and matching sombreros. On the other end of the kitsch scale is the work of Nikolai Syadristy, microminiature artist, whose exhibitions must be viewed through high-powered microscopes. He has created a golden chess set that sits on the head of a pin, a gathering of swallows on half of a poppy seed, and a biblical camel caravan located in the eye of a needle. Syadristy must first create the tools he uses to build his microminiatures, and they are so delicate that he works only between the beats of his heart.

I like these things not because they are precious but because they inspire me with wonder, they ask me to reenvision our relationship to space, they throw my own size into relief and make our human scale seem not preordained and ordinary but unlikely, arbitrary, and wondrous, too. I like hummingbirds because, after observing them, I'm returned to the world with a fresh sense of its mystery and a renewed appreciation for the fact that I'm part of it. Yes, they are small, and yes, they are beautiful, but, marvelously, they function, and they function marvelously. Like, say, a baby's hand. Like my baby's hand that, here in the thirty-ninth week, presses for a second against the taut shell of my belly, perfect outline, starfish on a cave wall, and then withdraws.

It's January. All is expectancy. To my south, the hummingbirds are eating, eating, ready for their difficult passage through the difficult night, ready to return to she who waits.

Beth Ann Fennelly

On "Salvos into the World of Hummers"

The Convergence of Subject and Style

In their 2004 text *Tell It Slant: Writing and Shaping Creative Nonfiction*, editors Brenda Miller and Suzanne Paola discuss a clever kind of essay that they term a "hermit crab essay" (a phrase that, incidentally, Dinty W. Moore references just a few essays ahead in this book). In short, a hermit crab essay is an essay that borrows its form from the thing it writes about, much like the hermit crab itself, who uses as its home a salvaged shell cast off by another creature. I like to experiment with forms for writing; I like the friction given off when a subject matter is explored against and through the restraints of form. In the past I've written poems in regular forms, such as the sonnet, and enjoyed discovering how writing in the tiny room of a sonnet forced me to felicities of language and thought I wouldn't have arrived at otherwise. But I've also written poems in discovered forms; one, for example, is in the form of a collection of Post-it notes; another includes a workable recipe for pesto.

This essay didn't want to come out as a straightforward narrative, and I think that's because the hummingbird itself is anything but straightforward. I'm attracted to the bird for its mystery and condensed power, and so I began to write about the hummingbird in small, condensed sections. I didn't worry too much about connecting the sections with neat transitions, because the birds themselves zing and zip and flash and disappear with so little transition. I brought in a lot of personal information—the addition we're building, my pregnancy—because hummers themselves seem to flit on the edges of the human world, both engaging with humans and being engaged by them, the objects of heavy anthropomorphism. If this essay exists on the "boundaries" of nonfiction, perhaps that's because it would be hard to categorize. The scientific material is accurate and writing the essay prompted me to do a lot of enjoyable research. But there are some dreamy, loose, poetic meditations that would keep this essay from finding a home in, say, a nature magazine or newspaper. Of course, there is a great pleasure to be had from the straightforward narrative that provides an arc, a beginning, middle, and end. This associative essay I've written forgoes that pleasure but hopefully provides a different kind of pleasure—that of various textures and tones rubbing up against each other. One section might instruct the reader in a cool new fact, one section I hope might make the reader smile (because hummingbirds are clownish at times, so I wanted some humor here); one section might prompt the reader to muse on nature's marvels.

Robin Hemley

Flagpole Wedding, Coshocton, Ohio, 1946

An Essay on Process

An old woman waits in her car at the deserted Coshocton county fairgrounds on this unseasonably warm January day. She's no one I know, no one important to this story, but I can't help noticing her and wondering what she's waiting for. I'm sure it's something completely mundane, but in my imagination I turn her into Lonnie Cosmar, who doesn't even live in Coshocton anymore, hasn't for many years, but she's got family here and maybe she's visiting them by coincidence on this day I'm visiting, trying to figure something out. We're both trying to figure something out, this white-haired woman soaking up the sun in the front seat of an old Ford Fairlane. She seems lost in reverie about the day sixty years earlier that she wed Mad Marshall Jacobs on a flagpole 176 feet above the grandstands here. I have the radio on, and maybe I've stopped really believing in coincidence a long time ago. Maybe only fate, after all, is real. The radio seems stuck on songs of breakup, one after another, my own personal soundtrack as I circle the fairgrounds trying to get a good angle to take a photograph that might approximate the angle of the photograph that Allen Grant took from the Goodyear Blimp on that June day in 1946. But I can't muster the Goodyear Blimp or all the resources of LIFE magazine. I only have a rental car, my own curiosity, and a frequent-flyer ticket I cashed in for this trip. My feet and my camera are firmly on the ground and every angle seems equally unsatisfying.

The road between Coshocton and Columbus tells another story, of billboards and reclaimed strip mines. Smokestacks announce the towns and sparse grass on hillsides through which black veins of coal peek and the billboards here caution and reassure alternately rather than advertise. Except for a building shaped like a picnic basket—its own billboard. This is southern Ohio, really a continuation, except for the name, of West Virginia, Appalachia. Not dirt poor but coal poor, and proud and patriotic. The billboards act as loose anchors for the people here, but maybe it's already too late, families frayed, towns preserved as they looked a hundred years ago, not out of historic preservation mindfulness but because no one has the money to build yet another mall. *Abstinence, 100% Effective. Whatever It Takes, Don't Let Your Friends Drop Out. Part-time Reservist, Full-time Hero. The Family That Prays Together, Stays Together*, and this last one reminds me of my own southern Ohio childhood, the road between Athens, Ohio, and Columbus, where each arm and leg of a roadside cross had a word painted on it—GET ... RIGHT ... WITH ... GOD—and then one day it only read GET ... WITH, and my family laughingly added a missing "IT," which seemed more appropriate to the late sixties, "IT" being whatever was hip and faddish, whatever was of the moment, because each cultural moment as we're passing through seems glorious and relevant and everlasting.

The war was over finally and America could breathe again and laugh. America could act silly and celebratory for as long as it took to wash away the memories of the Depression and war years, at least in 1946, before the new Cold War began and we found yet another enemy. Marshall Jacobs had been a daredevil for years, a man who could and would scale a building without a rope or a net on less than a dare. If the Coshocton High School football team scored a victory, he'd rush over to the courthouse and scale it in nineteen breathless minutes. It didn't even take that much for him to scale the courthouse or any other building he wanted to scale. In 1929 he and his brothers happened upon a crowd in downtown Coshocton watching a "Human Fly" scale the Oddfellows Building. The Human Fly's girlfriend was passing the hat to collect money for his feat, but Marshall wasn't impressed. "Any ten-year-old could climb that building," he told his brothers. "Here, hold my shoes for me." His brothers said, no, not any ten-year-old could climb that building, and no, they weren't going to hold his shoes, and besides, they knew Marshall had downed a couple of homebrews along with them at a friend's house, and they figured he was looped. "Tight," they called it. "You're tight and nobody's going to hold your shoes." So Marshall flagged down a friend in the crowd and said, "Hey, will you hold my shoes for me? I want to climb that building, but they think I'm tight. Do I look tight to you?"

Maybe his friend didn't care whether Marshall was tight or not, just wanted to see whether Marshall could do it or whether he'd bust his ass, either way a pretty good antidote for small-town boredom.

He held his shoes. The Human Fly was going up one corner and so Marshall decided to go up the other. He beat the Human Fly by five minutes and was waiting there for him when he arrived. The Human Fly said, "You trying to ruin my show?"

"You don't have a show," Marshall said as the Human Fly took out a little pad and did a headstand on it. Marshall asked to borrow the Fly's pad, but the Fly refused and climbed back down off the building. When Marshall got down, he found his friend and brothers had passed the hat for him and the good people of Coshocton had thrown in their nickels, dimes, and quarters, willingly, joyously, appreciatively for this young nut of a native son in their midst. When he counted it, he had sixty-five dollars.

But I wanted to know about the wedding on top of a flagpole 176 feet high, the world's largest flagpole. It wasn't Marshall I wanted to know about so much. It was his marriage. In 1995 I'd received that postcard of him and Lonnie Cosmar getting married up there. A friend had sent it to me to announce his own marriage, and I couldn't get over it. I still can't. The photo shows the couple dressed in full wedding regalia embracing on top of the pole, the bride's wedding train trailing over the pole, the houses of Coshocton and hills of Appalachia arrayed in the near distance below and behind them. I've never before seen such an iconic marriage photo—it suggested so much to me about both the obvious perils and the boldness and the hopefulness of that act, linking your life to that of another. As the years went on, I wanted to know who this couple was. To me, they weren't just an image. Of course they were real people, but who, and more importantly, what had happened to them? What had their marriage been like? They couldn't possibly still be alive. I didn't even have their names. The caption of the postcard read simply, "Flagpole Wedding, Coshocton, Ohio, 1946." But I wanted to find out one simple thing: had their marriage been a happy one?

Marshall's dad was a coal miner. For a while Marshall had been a hobo, eventually wound up as a steeplejack, could climb pretty much any building or structure, put up towers, tore them down, painted flagpoles, whatever needed doing at a height that most people couldn't take.

They say that being a Human Fly is all in the hands, but that's just reporter talk.

Marshall had had a couple of homebrews at a friend's house and he told his brother, "Why, I could do that better than him," and that's what he did. The Human Fly had a ten-minute head start and still Marshall beat him to the top. After that, nothing could keep Marshall on the ground. But the military rejected him, for high blood pressure of all things.

Few photos seem more compelling to me than a famous LIFE photo by Allen Grant of a couple standing in full wedding attire and kissing atop a flagpole towering over hills and houses in the blurry distance. The photo has been used in a film, Forget Paris, in the opening credits; Cingular wireless service wanted to use it once in an ad campaign; and a company in New York turned it into a postcard. That's how I first saw the photo. It came to me in 1995 as a wedding announcement from my friends Don and Lisa, who have been married ever since. I had spent eight and a half years by then in a marriage that I admit now I knew was a mistake on the honeymoon. Not that we were always miserable together, just not suited, but it's easier to justify the breakup of a marriage years later if you remember only the miserable moments. I remember the moment in Chicago, where we spent our honeymoon (not the most romantic destination, I admit, but we had a choice of a fancy honeymoon or a house and we chose the house). I was crossing the ———

A couple in full wedding attire stands atop a small platform on a nearly two-hundred-foot flagpole—they're kissing. In the background, trees and houses on a hill. The photo seems to say so much about marriage: the promise, the glory, the possible fatal missteps if you take one step in the wrong direction. The photo comes to me as a postcard in 1995, eight years into my first marriage. It's from my friend, Don Morrill, a poet, who told me that he and his wife, Lisa, might come up to visit us that summer if they could.

Don and Lisa never did come to visit that year or any other, but at least they managed to stay together, while my wife and I broke apart five years later. But I've kept the postcard all these years and wondered about this couple kissing on the flagpole. Who were they and what happened to them? Did they have a happy marriage? The only clue the postcard gives me is a location. "Flagpole Wedding, Coshocton, Ohio, 1946."

One of these days, I tell myself, I'm going to Coshocton to find out.

She's just a grandma now. It's hard to imagine her on a flagpole.

I received the postcard from my friend, poet Don Morrill, eleven years ago. It showed a couple ———

Robin Hemley

On "Flagpole Wedding, Coshocton, Ohio, 1946: An Essay on Process"

Transitioning from Notes to Novel

My essay takes the form of some early notes on my project on the flag-pole wedding. At first glance, even second and third, this might seem like a cheat or a dodge, using my notes and calling them an essay on process. But I can't imagine a more pertinent essay on process and blurring than this, at least for my purposes.

I write both fiction and nonfiction, and so part of my process is try-ing to decide where my project fits. I first started "Flagpole Wedding" as an essay, but as I progressed I wanted to inhabit the lives of the characters. Mad Marshall Jacobs in particular intrigued me, and I tried to write a research-based essay that would incorporate his thoughts and dialogue based on extensive research I did on his life. My model was Jo Ann Beard's masterful essay "Werner," in which she writes in third person limited point of view about an artist in New York City. Her essay was rather audacious in that it read like a short story, yet it was based on her interviews with Werner. I read this essay first in *The Best American Essays*, and it remains one of the most boundary-busting essays I've read.

In my case, I interviewed Lonnie Cosmar, the woman on the flagpole, and went to Coshocton and researched the flagpole wedding and the life of Jacobs. When I thought I was finished with the piece, I sent it to a few friends, including David Shields, an old friend of mine, who told me he thought the piece was more of a short story. Until then, I hadn't thought of the piece as fiction.

A little confused, I brought the piece with me to Australia, where I was doing a retreat with several Australian writers. I showed the piece to several of the writers, including Cate Kennedy, the eminent novelist and short story writer. Cate thought the piece was the beginning of a novel.

So that's where I am right now with this project, in a space between genres, full of conjecture about form. The creative process in any case is long and sometimes frustrating. The only other novel I've written and published in my career likewise began in a confused and protean form, first as a failed short story with multiple points of view, eventually morphing into a novel. While I'm not certain where "Flagpole Wedding" will go from here, the notes that I've presented as my essay on process are my most honest expression of the way in which I work as a writer, dancing around the subject, stepping inside and outside of the story, always triangulating what I know and what I hope to discover in writing the piece. It's not so important to me that the finished project fit neatly into one genre or another. Ideally, I'd love for the project to be a kind of essayistic novel along the lines of a Sebald novel—that's probably where the project is ultimately headed because I don't think that a tightly constructed plot would accomplish what I want to accomplish, which is to investigate marriage, both personally and culturally, using the flagpole wedding as the fulcrum of the essay/novel/story.

Naomi Kimbell

Whistling in the Dark

Introduction

Insubstantial phenomena are well-documented and culturally universal occurrences (Bisher 1972, Cayce 1967, Langley 1972, Moody 1987, Yarbro 1986). But the sciences have yet to acknowledge the verifiable, though often nonreplicable, experiences of individuals and groups who have witnessed seemingly inexplicable, insubstantial events.[1] This denial of insubstantial realities has fostered an unhealthy arrogance in the scientific research community (personal opinion, Kimbell 2007), particularly among those in the fields of psychiatry and psychology. Thus it is my goal that this treatise will provide a counterargument to the diagnosis "psychotic" that has been misapplied to individuals who experience insubstantial phenomena. Furthermore, I will prove that insubstantial phenomena can be verified through a process of scientific inquiry based upon the Socratic method, which will remove said experiences, once and for all, from the catchall category of "psychosis," thus freeing thousands from the stigma of having been labeled "psychotic" by well-meaning, though careless and insensitive, health-care professionals.

Method

What is proof? Proof is indisputable. It is irrefutable. It is absolute *and* it is in the pudding, as well as eggs, sugar, and milk, breadcrumbs if it is a bread pudding, and for that matter also suet (rendered animal fat) and fruit (Rombauer and Becker 1975).

1. Jesus in the tortilla, Mexico, 1984.

Like Schrödinger's Cat (1935/1980), the pudding is both proved and unproven before it is eaten.[2] It exists in both states until we sample it. Similarly, "psychosis" exists both as a thought disorder and as an unmeasured, insubstantial phenomenon until the symptoms afflicting the subject are vetted. The subsequent information derived from this thorough process of inquiry gives the researcher the ability to distinguish between the two possible conclusions, thus correctly diagnosing the subject's symptoms and acting accordingly. If the vetting reveals that the subject is indeed psychotic, public mental health professionals or a private-pay psychiatrist should be notified immediately. If, however, the vetting reveals an alternate truth, established best practices should be used in order to treat and eliminate the symptoms/affliction.[3]

Biases

Before proceeding further, I will identify the biases that may or may not affect the conclusions of this paper. Bias unidentified can produce findings that, frankly, misrepresent the truth, "prove" a specious point, or in fact, invent systems of belief that influence generations of "rational," mainstream thought.[4] Thus, in order to avoid that common pitfall, the

2. A good overview of Schrödinger's Cat can be found in *Prince of Darkness*, a film by John Carpenter about the incarnation of Satan's son on earth.
3. Depending on the manifestation of the insubstantial phenomena, best practices will include a wide variety of possible responses. There is the "do no harm" response, which is a proactive way of saying do nothing, especially if the phenomenon is merely annoying and poses no threat; exorcism may be indicated if the phenomenon manifests as "internal," but only if one can find a reliable practitioner; and one may employ a theoretical physicist, a faith healer, or both if the phenomenon seems bizarre, evil, and intent upon doing more damage than a simple possession or other discrete event.
4. Psychoanalysis, string theory, relativity, trickle-down economics, NAFTA, modernity, post-modernity, heterodoxy, orthodoxy, anarchy, libertarianism, secular humanism, religion (all), anachronism, post-anachronism, structural anachronism, and, of course, post-structural anachronism, wave theory, particle theory, nature vs. nurture, and Karl Rove.

list of identified biases regarding this treatise follows:

1. I have a psychiatric diagnosis of bipolar disorder, which I accept, and am currently recovering from a "break."
2. Some of the phenomena I experience as a result of my illness fall into the category of "psychotic features," but other experiences, though insubstantial and similar in form to hallucinations, I believe to be "real."
3. I also believe that "reality" is the creation of the observer. Each of us experiences the "real" differently and I have not found anyone who can satisfactorily define it for me.
4. Because of this, I have had difficult relationships with both psychiatrists and psychologists in that we often disagree about objective reality. They claim there is one; I ask them to prove it.
5. And, though I try not to discuss it for a variety of reasons, mainly because both the phrase and the phenomenon have become commodified, *I see dead people.*

The Problem[5]

I occasionally see people on my couch that others do not see. Mental health professionals have called this experience "psychosis," but I disagree that I am psychotic and that, in fact, all insubstantial manifestations are hallucinations. By way of proving my point (the point that I am not psychotic), I offer this: psychotic people rarely function well in society.[6] They rarely hold jobs. Whereas I both function well, for the most part, *and* have a job.[7] Yes, admittedly, I *do* have a mental

---

5. For those of you in motivational speaking, retreat facilitation, upper management, human resources, and guidance counseling, I do mean *problem*, not *challenge* or *opportunity*.
6. Cassandra in Euripedes's "Trojan Women," 415 BCE.
7. If the reader would like a copy of my résumé, ordering instructions are located at the end of this document.

illness, but I have insight into this fact and I have learned, with the help of trained professionals, to discern the feelings, actions, and thoughts that are products of my illness from those that are "normal" or "real." The people on my couch are real. They have always been there in one form or another and no amount of counseling or medicine will remedy the situation.

The Backstory

The phenomenon of insubstantive experience first manifested in my life in the midseventies. As I was a creative child, my parents disregarded my assertions that there were additional people in the house as products of an overactive imagination. My mother started giving me extra vitamins, and a nightlight was installed in my room.[8] This did not stop the phenomenon; it only prevented me from seeing what I knew was still there (though my parents remained adamant that I was only imagining things). Now, as an adult, I am cautious not to dismiss out of hand things that are not easily explained. I work hard to be reflective before passing judgment on a specter, a bump in the night, or a tug on my collar from an invisible hand. True, some of these occurrences have turned out to be symptoms—perhaps I have forgotten to take my medication, I've changed my diet, or I have gone without sleep for several days—but many occurrences have stood up to the Socratic method, thus proving that additional, visually elusive people are not manifestations of my illness but rather have lived and continue to live in my house.

Sometimes in the dark, on my way to the kitchen for a glass of water, I see silent gloomy shapes sitting on the couch, perhaps with their hands folded.[9] Their dark forms are nearly completely still, but

---

8. She gave me niacin amide, having once read in an Adele Davis book that this particular B vitamin cured schizophrenia.
9. *See* is used loosely here.

they are there—is one tapping a thumb on a knee? Or picking at lint with the slightest movement of the index finger? I believe I might have heard a yawn, once, and that made me think of purgatory and doctors' offices—*these people are bored.*[10]

Some Facts

Not all matter is visible (Ginzberg 2007). Matter cannot be destroyed (Lederman and Teresi 2006). Matter is a wave (Grand 2001).

The universe is filled with matter that cannot be seen.[11] Dark matter, the stuff that physicists believe makes up the majority of the mass in the universe, has been observed by astronomers, who have recorded its effects on the rotation and velocity of galaxies (Wikipedia 2007). Dark matter must be observed by its *effects* because, similar to the people on my couch, it neither emits nor reflects enough electromagnetic energy to be observed directly. One can see only what it leaves in its wake—hairbrushes that go missing, bus passes that vanish, a broken mirror, lids off the jelly jars, crumbs in the butter, and galactic rotational speeds in excess of what the observable matter predicts.

Also intriguing is the premise that matter cannot be destroyed. It can only be converted to energy. This is the work of particle accelerators and particle physicists and it really has no direct bearing on this paper, per se. But I include it because I think this axiom provides a pretty good rationalization for the existence of ghosts.[12] And, though I acknowledge this is tangential, I'll ask the reader to consider DEATH.

I posit that death is a sort of natural particle accelerator, albeit a slow one. As the body decays, energy is released. That energy can dissipate, mutate, ascend, descend, or reassemble into the shape to which it had become accustomed—the body—thus becoming a ghost. I am not

10. And idle hands are the devil's playthings.
11. Higgs bosons.
12. Another phenomenon often dismissed as a product of hysteria or psychosis.

asserting that the people on my couch are ghosts, however. Ghosts tend to moan, point, and whine; the people in my house are silent, and I have no connection with the recently dead, which, I believe, is a prerequisite for a haunting (Auerbach 2003, Steiger 2003).

My favorite fact of the three that began this section is also tangential: matter is a wave (Grand 2001).[13] In his book *Creation: Life and How to Make It*, Steve Grand says that matter is a disturbance in the fabric of space rather than a superimposition of particles upon it. Some of this matter is visible. Some of it is not. So, perhaps this tangent has been useful, having led the discussion back to Ginzberg: *not all matter is visible*—and all things are possible.

Measurement[14]

13. The *DSM-IV* has some interesting things to say about tangents and tangential thinking. Personally, I think of tangents as a mark of intelligence and creativity, though for the most part, tangents are categorized by mental health professionals as *symptoms*.

14. Currently, there is no measuring device on the market equal to the pursuit of detecting insubstantial phenomena other than the six senses. Current levels of technology simply haven't advanced far enough to be truly useful to the needs of psychology, psychiatry, and parapsychology. Particle accelerators, as yet, have only revealed information regarding the visible universe; none have produced the elusive Higgs boson, and as I understand it, scientists are still far from nailing that discovery. The United States might have been a contender for the prize of First Documented Higgs Boson, but funding was eliminated in favor of the Superconducting Supercollider and momentum has stalled.

    However, some hope exists in an international community of scientists on the border between France and Switzerland who have recently gotten their own supercollider on line (the Large Hadron Collider). But I haven't heard the ETA on the arrival of a Higgs boson, nor have the scientists announced plans for the development of useful, aftermarket technologies that would assist in detecting infiltrations of dark matter into daily life. Needless to say, this is frustrating because little store is placed in the accuracy of the six senses as a measuring device, given that the senses are almost wholly subjective, thus rendering the results of their measurements easily dismissible by those whom I wish to persuade.

The Vetting

I first learned the word *vet* when I was thirty-one. I had to look it up and found this definition: to appraise, verify, or check for accuracy, authenticity, validity, etc. (Dictionary.com 2008). I immediately saw the usefulness of this word and have been saving it. The opportunity to vet does not often occur in the daily grind. People have no patience for vetting. Similarly, people have little or no patience for the Socratic method as a tool for vetting, as Socrates was misfortuned to learn.[15] So I knew that if I ever wanted to use the word or, in fact, if I ever wished to vet, I would need to wait for a time when both the word and the process were wholly appropriate, timely, and served a higher purpose. That time is here: I wish to vet the insubstantial phenomenon of visually elusive people on my couch using the Socratic method, my six senses, and any such help that theoretical physics, cosmology, and parapsychology can provide in order to establish the validity of my assertion that the people on my sofa are, in fact, real.

Tools, Weights, and Measures

Touch, taste, hearing, sight, smell—these senses are merely physical and irrelevant to this process of discovery. The sixth sense, however, is an instrument of heightened perception; it pricks up your ears, raises goose bumps on your arms, draws the air from your lungs and the bile from your bravery.[16] It is both the perfect device of detection and the perfect instrument of measurement. Since my diagnosis I have learned to use it as a way of distinguishing reality from symptom. My psychologist says she would like me to use my mind to do that, but

---

15. Hemlock.
16. The sixth sense is often viewed with disdain because of its abuse by Hollywood film-makers, Pentecostal evangelists, and animal whisperers. Nevertheless, it remains one of the most powerful tools of observation and measurement available today.

some phenomena simply defy the rational limitations of the mind and one must resort to other human qualities in order to sort it all out.

For example, when I walk through my house at night, I get the fantods in my living room.[17] No other room produces this response. The feeling is visceral, primordial. Something is there in the dark, on the sofa. If I ignore the feeling and go about my business, I still *feel* the watching. However, if I turn to look, it is the forest at night, black and impossible to see, the trees are there — are not there — one can tell only because they blot out the sky.

If I probe this first feeling, the gut reaction to the darkness that masks itself as night, my initial questions are, Why should I feel this way about my sofa if there is truly nothing there? Am I not an evolved being? Do I not have reflexes and reactions that have been honed millennia after millennia to warn me of danger and doom? Should I dismiss the fantods simply because it doesn't seem conventionally reasonable that there are people on the sofa whom I cannot see? I think the obvious answer is, No, the fantods should not be dismissed. That leaves us with the obvious question, What now?

Next in the vetting, if we are not going to dismiss the fantods, is to measure their intensity using the Fantod Scale Kolor Swatch System®.[18]

17. *Fantods* is Victorian for the *creeps.*
18. The Fantod Scale is divided into categories or levels called "sensory tiers." The sensory tiers are numbered one through six, each with an associated color in a Kolor Swatch System®. (The Kolor Swatch System® is new and represents an attempt to keep the sensory tier scale consistent with other warning systems currently in use. However, in order to distinguish the scale from the more common alert systems and colors, the subcommittee worked to develop this system in keeping with fashion and the expectations of a discerning public.)

The Fantod Scale Kolor Swatch System®
Level One — Flutter®
Level Two — Wicker Basket®
Level Three — Always Appropriate®

When interacting with insubstantial phenomena, intensity often equates to proximity.

For example, when I am standing in my kitchen with a wall between me and my sofa, my sixth sense remains at rest and does not register on the scale. Now, if I enter the living room and face the sofa directly, I feel a bit uneasy—say, Level Two, or *Wicker Basket*®. But if I face the sofa obliquely to head down the hall, the anxiety increases. If I continue to pass, turning my back to the sofa, a swelling begins inside, like a balloon inflating in my chest, then tremors and a desire to run overwhelm me.[19] This feeling qualifies as about a three on the Fantod Scale Kolor Swatch System®, or *Always Appropriate*®, so I know I am not really in danger but I do have the heebie-jeebies. If I try another experiment, one in which I approach the sofa directly, the results are quite different. The first step shoots the anxiety right to Level Four, or *Coup d'état*®, but it hovers there, steady—I'm pretty scared but not in any real danger. If I'm willing to endure *Girl's Best Friend*®, I can actually sit on the sofa where I believe the people to be, though it's hard to

---

Level Four—Coup d'état®
Level Five—Girl's Best Friend®
Level Six—Misty Dawn®

A Fantod Scale reaction of Level One, or *Flutter*®, is equivalent to the feeling one gets when entering an old house for the first time. Maybe you'd get a little chill and say something like, "Boy! This place feels weird." But after a while the feeling would pass and your sixth sense activity would no longer register as measurable in your physical body.

From *Flutter*® the levels progress through the Kolor Swatch System®, each gradation a richer hue, becoming increasingly uncomfortable until death presents itself as a possibility. For example, Level Six, *Misty Dawn*®, also known as the "Screaming Fantods," is nearly always fatal, so if you experience the agitating sensation of mordant fear, it's probably best to extricate yourself from whatever wacky situation you've gotten yourself into. Seriously.

19. If you learn nothing else from this paper, learn this: don't run.

relax and it seems a little weird, you know, sitting on someone's lap. So, rather than endure it and hover near the edge of the diaphanous malignancy of Misty Dawn®, I have simply turned my sofa over to the people I can't see and, in fact, I've discovered that I have very little need to go into the living room at all. I prefer the kitchen.[20]

20. Conclusion

I am pretty satisfied that I have made my point and I feel it's time to let my colleagues in the nether-fields (parapsychology 'n' theoretical physics) carry the scientific torch. I am not used to so much linear thinking and scientific methodology. Suffice it to say, I have demonstrated that not all hallucinations are hallucinations; some things that others cannot see are real. The Fantod Scale Kolor Swatch System® is one way of determining whether or not something you can't see is real because it uses proximity to elicit reaction. If something is just a hallucination, it wouldn't matter how close one is to the phenomenon because the hallucination is all-encompassing and does not travel along rational vectors.

Critics of this treatise might easily find flaw in my method and conclusions: Did I ever really use the Socratic method? Did I ever really vet my thesis? Did I adequately describe the Fantod Scale Kolor Swatch System® and locate it within the history and practice of scientific measurement? I suspect the answer to all these is, No. I did not. But, much like a grant-funded scientist, I don't really care. I am tired of trying to convince others that I know what is real and what is not real. I am also tired of confessing my symptoms, qualifying what I say, and prefacing sentences with, "I know this sounds crazy, but . . ." And, anyhow, I don't *have* a grant or an oversight committee or even constituents, so I can pretty much conclude whatever I want.

Last week I was afraid of my houseplants—it was nuts, I know, but still, they scared me. It's like they *knew* I wasn't watering them often enough or something—and the medication I take didn't help. It can't relieve all the symptoms; some will always reappear. I have bipolar disorder and for my whole life I have been trying to understand things in the same way everyone else seems to. It wasn't until I was thirty-six that I finally understood why I couldn't ever do it . . . oh, and if you still want a copy of my résumé, write to the publisher. I've given them my permission to mail it out. But it won't tell you anything. I am much more than my résumé. Much more than the sum of my parts. Much, much more. You can't even imagine. Not really. You'd have to meet me to know and the publisher does not have permission to give out my phone number or address. And I don't blog. No *way*. Not *this* girl.

References

American Psychiatric Association. (2000). *Diagnostic and Statistical Manual of Mental Disorders* (4th ed.). Washington DC: American Psychiatric Association.

Auerbach, L. (2003). *How to Investigate the Paranormal.* Berkeley CA: Ronin.

Bisher, F. (1972). *Strange but True Baseball Stories.* New York: Random House.

Bogdan, R. (1990). *Freakshow: Presenting Human Oddities for Amusement and Profit.* Chicago: University of Chicago Press.

Cayce, E. (1967). *Reincarnation.* New York: Warner Books.

Concordance Bible. (1973). *God's Word for a New Age.* New York: Churches of Christ in the United States of America, American Bible Society.

Descartes, R. (1996). *Meditations on First Philosophy.* Cambridge: Cambridge University Press.

Euripides. (1960). *Euripides: Ten Plays.* New York: Bantam Classics.

Ginzberg, V. (2007). *Prime Elements of Ordinary Matter, Dark Matter and Dark Energy: Beyond Standard Model and String Theory.* Boca Raton FL: Universal.

Grand, S. (2001). *Creation: Life and How to Make It.* Cambridge: Harvard University Press.

Homer. (1961). *The Iliad of Homer* (R. Lattimore, Trans.). Chicago: University of Chicago Press.

Hume, D. (1999). *An Enquiry Concerning Human Understanding.* Oxford: Oxford University Press.

Jones, M. D. (2006). *PSIence: How New Discoveries in Quantum Physics and New Science May Explain the Existence of Paranormal Phenomena.* Franklin Lakes NJ: New Page Books.

Langley, N. (1972). *Edgar Cayce on Reincarnation.* New York: Warner.

Lederman, L., and Teresi, D. (2006). *The God Particle.* New York: Mariner Books.

Moody, R. A., Jr. (1987). *Elvis after Life.* New York: Bantam Books.

Radin, D. (2006). *Entangled Minds: Extrasensory Experiences in a Quantum Reality.* Cyberspace: Paraview Pocket Books.

Rombauer, I. von Starkloff, and Becker, M. Rombauer. (1975). *The Joy of Cooking.* New York: Bobbs-Merrill.

Schrödinger, E. (1980). "The Present Situation in Quantum Mechanics: A Translation of Schrödinger's 'Cat Paradox' Paper" (J. D. Trimmer, Trans.). *Proceedings of the American Philosophical Society,* 124, 323–38. (Originally published as "Die gegenwärtige Situation in der Quantenmechanik." *Naturwissenschaften, 23,* 1935, 807–12, 823–28, 844–49.)

Shiner, L. (1993). *Glimpses.* New York: Avon Books.

Steiger, B. (2003). *Real Ghosts, Restless Spirits, and Haunted Places.* Canton MI: Visible Ink Press.

Wikipedia. (2007). It is what it is.

Yarbro, C. Q. (1986). *More Messages from Michael.* New York: Berkeley Books.

Naomi Kimbell

On "Whistling in the Dark"

When Telling Lies Reveals Truth

"Whistling in the Dark" came to life spontaneously. I had a story to tell but until I wrote the first line, I didn't know how to tell it. It is a story about the despair associated with the experience of being a person with mental illness and being objectified by care providers—in my case, mental health-care professionals. I ended up telling this story as satire, something that occurred accidentally in the first few lines but as I began to bend the sciences and scientific writing to my will, I knew I was on to something; I saw that the voice I had chosen not only fit the purpose of the story but also allowed the intensity of my emotions to be more readable because writing, in my opinion, is not complete without both a writer *and* a reader. Writing, put simply, is communication, and without the reader I'm just talking to myself and that is a symptom of psychosis, something I try to avoid.

In order to achieve this dialogue between reader and writer, these problems of readability really need to be figured out. I think of it as throwing the reader a bone. Thus, the first and most important gesture a writer can make to the reader is letting him or her in on the joke. Right up front, the reader knows "Whistling" parodies scientific language because I use both the tone and structure easily found in science journals; I don't reinvent the wheel because structure, in an essay like this, is the only real thing the reader can hang onto as I lead him or her through a maze of false facts as well as the deeper, emotional story I want to develop: in the weeks and months before I wrote "Whistling" I was diagnosed as psychotic and medicated for it, and I became very sick, but I still wrote. I developed a contrary, and even fictional, argument against the medical canon in order to save something of myself that I could recognize. The structure I chose helped me do that.

Now, with the structure in place, I used fiction to write a *nonfiction* narrative. I made stuff up. I lied. I used endnotes with further lies and I pushed the limits of veracity even further by monkeying with the citations page, though I used APA formatting. This formality of the structure juxtaposed with both truth and untruth was necessary for my critique of mental health-care providers because it is the same form to which I was subjected. For instance, I have literally watched a provider pick up a *Diagnostic and Statistical Manual* (DSM-IV) while speaking with me, find a diagnosis that more or less fit their assumptions, and then write a prescription with no further discussion. For all I know, my diagnosis came from a footnote and my lived experience was brushed aside.

Because I had suddenly gone from a regular person with problems to one of the "mentally ill," I lost a lot of confidence in my writing abilities. Some feedback I received from colleagues compounded this fear when their critique of my work suggested my essays were too emotional and too raw to read. Likely they were, and this caused my belief in myself as a writer to deteriorate even further. However, as a natural contrarian, I didn't quit. Rather, I pushed the limits of nonfiction even further and wrote pages and pages of experiments. Tomes of footnotes never made it into the final essay; nothing was sacred and I wasn't afraid to cut and cut again. The lesson here: even fenceless essays need to be edited.

During the editing process I drew on pop culture to nestle the story into a comfortable "reality" in which the audience could participate: films such as *The Sixth Sense*, spiritual experiences such as sightings of Jesus, and even President Bush's color-coded threat level scale, though I chose to use paint chip colors instead. Once I thought I was finished, I saw that I had put together a piece of nonfiction that was simultaneously wholly inaccurate and the truest thing I have ever written. The truth, in this case, is in both the form and the appropriation of scientific language to explore my suspicion that facts are subject to change without notice, especially when talking about people. My interpretation of the facts, a subjective interpretation, can be as right as another, and so the truth is not in the facts, it is in me, or to be trendy, in the observer. By stretching my boundaries as a writer I developed both my skills and a renewed belief in my work and its purpose.

I even came up with a phrase I tell my students as they tackle a new project: write bravely. It is better to be brave in your work and miss the mark than it is to be safe. This is what it means to dispense with convention, and this is what it is to be a writer.

Kim Dana Kupperman

71 Fragments for a Chronology of Possibility

so much depends
upon

a red wheel
barrow . . .
William Carlos Williams

1.

So much depends upon how you might first touch my hand, not by accident, but with hunger and purpose, as if you were staking a claim, as if such desire might be slaked.

2.

So much depends on my letting time unfold a story (something I am not good at doing, perhaps because I can imagine almost instantly the narrative, from inception to conclusion); and so much depends on my consigning this ache to a subterranean cache of aches and my making a point to pretend that I will come to the end of this yearning.

Title after Michael Haneke's 71 Fragments of a Chronology of Chance. Thanks to James Baldwin, the Beatles, William Coperthwaite, e. e. cummings, Annie Dillard, Kit Hathaway, Werner Herzog, bell hooks, Jack London, Gabriel García Márquez, Edgar Allan Poe, Elizabeth Smart, Dustin Beall Smith, James Sprouse, Wallace Stevens, Dylan Thomas, Henry David Thoreau, Linda Underhill, E. B. White, William Carlos Williams, Robert Wilson, Virginia Woolf.

3.

So much depends upon where you are when the tornado (howling like the freight train you were warned to listen for) rips through your neighborhood and your consciousness to cut a swath through the trees, much like a giant might, though publicly you would swear you didn't believe in giants even if privately you are certain they exist.

4.

Even if it's not obvious, so much depends upon how the cat sits with his tail curled up under his cheek, and how the dog circles the spot in which she will lie.

5.

Then there's water: so much depends on whether it is salted or fresh, if it rises in a flood or is nonexistent, if it collects in a rain barrel, flows or drips from a faucet, or if the Rebecca who draws it from a well and offers it to the stranger passing through the desert is really an anonymous waitress filling a glass.

6.

So much depends upon a red-and-black bowl, the wooden chopsticks beside it, the white linen napkin still folded on the table, and how we wait, in silence, for a guest to arrive.

7.

Today I believe that so much depends on whether I can summon who I once was to play the role of who I am now.

8.

I never realized how much depends upon the hierarchies of rocks and soil, minerals and gems, ice and clouds; if you really can teach a stone to talk, or if the rain does indeed have such small hands.

9.

As I write this, I realize that so much depends upon
how much
or how little
or what, if anything,
you will read between the lines, if crypsis exists anymore in this tell-all Age of the Word, or if nuance still has some purchase.

10.

So much depends on moonlight, whether its brightness incites me to frenzy instead of sleep, or if it is as absent as your hand on my shoulder, an emptiness that also keeps me awake.

11.

There was a time I thought that a lot depended on the distinctions between *forge* and *forgery*; now I see that such differences do not matter much anymore.

12.

So much depends upon how you looked at me from across the room or how you said good-bye before I was ready, or how I never said what I was really thinking and that I was really thinking about all the years of never saying what I was thinking and how they added up to the one true thing I should have said.

13.

If you think it matters, then it's true that so much depends on what we see when we look out our respective windows: snow there, maples on the verge of budding; sunshine here, maples leafed out.

14.

So much depends on my advance, your retreat.

15.

So much depends on the kind of paper these words are written on, the color of the ink, knowing that each letter was originally fashioned by my hand, that it took a lifetime to learn to shape these letters into these words in just this way, and that it was your invitation that brought me here to this singular moment.

16.

So much depends upon a threadbare black jacket with a yellow star sewn into its lapel, and whether someone in your family may have worn such an article of clothing.

17.

So much depends on the difference between living lives of quiet desperation or living lives of frantic silences.

18.

So much depends on taking a day off to sleep in late, remembering a dream, lingering on iced-in February mornings over coffee and oranges, and contemplating all the ways to look at a blackbird.

19.

I tell you, and I hope you're listening: so much depends on the birth and death of random curiosities.

20.

Just the other day, it occurred to me that where I stand today depends upon the sacrifices I was willing to make, the ones I can never regret and all those I do, even if I don't acknowledge regretting them.

21.

You see the young man, the young woman; you see all they might become if they make the decisions they're told they shouldn't make, and you want to proclaim that so much depends on teaching to transgress and getting it right.

22.

So much will depend upon what you see when you finally look deeply into my face, these upturned palms, past the aging of my skin and beyond my toenails and into the dark heart of the story I long to tell you.

23.

So much depends on whether it was Penn Station or Grand Central, if I sat down and wept there, or if I simply bought a ticket and boarded the train.

24.

For Lily and Rosemary, a lot depended on the Jack of Hearts (for Robert Zimmerman, so much depended on Bob Dylan); in turn, everything depends on luck, fortune, and chance; on being in the right place at the right time or in the wrong place at the right time, the right place at the wrong time, or the wrong place at the wrong time.

25.

So much depends upon where tears go once they have fallen.

26.

So much depends on the books lost when the Great Library at Alexandria burned, and even more depends on the people, the animals, the artifacts — the evidence of great knowledge — that perished in that mythic fire.

27.

My father taught me that so much depends upon the people you know and how much you trust them; from my mother I learned that so much depends on whether those you love die before you've said everything you need to tell them.

28.

So much depends upon when you pick the fig, how you bite into it, and what you do with the fig leaf.

29.

So much depends on how we interpret the bear in the dream, the owl flying overhead, the milk snake in the woodshed, the rabbits in the field running circles around one another.

30.

So much depends on keeping a straight face when you can barely keep from laughing.

31.

Please don't hang up the phone when I finally tell you what I've been thinking, that so much depends on what it will feel like when, without question, regret, doubt, or anything arresting this moment, you rest your head in my lap.

32.

So much depends on a clutch of blue eggs, the Bantam hens broody upon them.

33.

It wasn't me who first had the inkling that so much depends on the little language that lovers use and the world being round like an orange and words living in the mind, not the dictionary.

34.

So much depends on the hour we turn off the lamps, and so much depends on the shadows cast by light not yet extinguished.

35.

So much depends upon photosynthesis, hypothesis, antithesis.

36.

Amole es geven: this is a true story, my heart: so much depends on the *lamed vov*, the thirty-six unknown-even-to-themselves saints who keep the world intact by being kind and just and uncompromising in their goodness.

37.

So much depends on independence.

38.

Any living thing can tell you how much depends upon fertilization, viability, and the more complicated and messy work of living up to the subsequent combination of DNA that uncoils.

39.

So much depends on mystery, being surprised, looking at things with a different perspective.

40.

Yes: wolf, coyote, fox—so much depends upon the call of the wild, its invasion into the silence of my nights, the way it rocks the little boat of my cerebellum.

41.

Eventually you learn just how much depends on how and when your parents die, if they depart intestate or have bound you with ironclad wills, if the dynasty they bequeath can be sustained or if it is more likely to crumble, if they ask you (or not) to be executor, pallbearer, health-care surrogate, or have power of attorney, if they rage or pass gently into a day or a night, if their final instructions freeze in their throats, if you can hear them whispering recipes for peach cobbler or directions to the bank vault once they've departed.

42.

So much depends on the cardinal at the bird feeder, his alarm of red feathers, the female he is trying to coax into coupling, the nest they will construct twig by twig, whether their young will return here next year, and if the tree on whose limbs he is perching now will still be standing or if it will have been cut down or struck by lightning.

43.

So much depends upon a well-crafted plot, though some author/ities might tell you that fiction is irrelevant in these days of truth and non-truth telling.

44.

I hate admitting this, but so much depends on money, even though I'm certain it can't buy you love.

45.

So much depends on eros, divinity, the sublime, and how we navigate the ecologies of passion, faith, and mystery.

46.

It's impossible to list all the things that depend on insects.

47.

In the Mongolia of my quotidian reveries, I saw how much depends on what kind of shaman you think you can be and the type of medicine woman I may become.

48.

So much depends upon how many shade trees are left once the tree cutting begins.

49.

So much depends on uncertainty: If you look at me a certain way, will it change me? If you know a lot about where I am, you probably won't know anything about the velocity that conveyed me here, and if you know exactly how long it took me to arrive, chances are you'll be uncertain about where I'm really standing.

50.

So much depends upon your browsing the scent of my sun-kissed skin and the sibilance of those words as they utter themselves in your mind.

51.

So much depends on the fallacy of memory, the wreckage of truth we conceal, the lies we do not tell.

52.

So much depends on what is misunderstood, left unclarified, or abandoned to the archives of mishandled information.

53.

Here's a bulletin to heed: so much depends upon where you'll be when the war starts and whether you'll know how to use that gun.

54.

So much depends on the work of squirrels, the number of acorns they buried last fall and how hungry they will be once the snows melt.

55.

So much depends upon synthesis, abstraction, and the clarity requisite to envision imaginary numbers.

56.

In spite of skepticism or the inability of others to suspend disbelief, I believe that so much depends on words spelled by spiders, the collaboration between bats and birds, the songs of bees, the dreams of fish.

57.

So much depends on whether we give in to indifference.

58.

So much depends upon whether how I imagine you is real or if who you actually are is a figment of my dreaming imagination.

59.

So much depends on the rightness of the broom, how it is held while sweeping and, as it pushes across the floorboards, if it sounds akin to the brushing of coarse hair, or whether it resonates more like small waves lapping a wooden shore.

60.

Imagine the conversation between Galileo and Copernicus, and how they might have debated what depends upon the lengthening and shortening of days and how we interpret the sun's rising and setting, what we make of eclipses, or conjunctions of Venus and Mars, and how we live the unequal hours.

61.

So much depends upon what you can get away with stealing or copying and if the theft is considered a restoration or a resurrection.

62.

So much depends on grammar, context, revision.

63.

So much depends on the democracy of an axe, how the lumber is hewn, and who helps you stack the woodpile.

64.

Tea parties aside, so much depends on how quietly or boisterously a revolution starts.

65.

So much depends on the translations we make, not necessarily of words, but of tone, inflection, gesture, cadence.

66.

So much depends on the number six (the only number that is both the sum and the product of three consecutive positive numbers), including hexagons, Stars of David, the month of June, the planet Venus, the degrees of separation between us.

67.

So much depends on how eager you are to feel my breath behind your ear.

68.

So much depends on the poetry of indecision and the prosody of choice.

69.

So much depends on whether you choose to turn six upside down to make a nine.

70.

So much depends upon whether you think of ants as friends or vermin, or if you rescue the mouse your cat has cornered.

71.

So much depends on how fragments coincide, are catalogued, and how they repeat, intersect, or offer some semblance of forgiveness, solace, a chance at humility, a way into a telltale heart.

Kim Dana Kupperman

On "71 Fragments for a Chronology of Possibility"

An Eight-Fragment, Five-Paragraph Essay

I. Introduction

Thesis statement: An essay coalesces from ordinary events.

II. Body

A. *Things Come Together of Their Own Accord*

In the fall of 2009 I watched every film by Michael Haneke that I could rent from Netflix.[1] The final movie in this marathon was *71 Fragments of a Chronology of Chance*, the third in Haneke's Glaciation Trilogy, so named because the three films document, as he says, "the coldness of the society in which we live." The titular echo of Haneke's film, whose primary concern is isolation, and in particular, the kind that originates in fragmentation and devolves into violence, provides both an anchor and a juxtaposition for the speaker in the essay, whose mind meanders far and wide, always returning to address an unrequited yearning, which is also a form of isolation, but which the speaker perceives (perhaps incorrectly) as the seed of love and thus an antidote to both fragmentation and isolation.

---

1. This enterprise was as intellectually and artistically fulfilling as it was emotionally exhausting.

B. No Ideas But in Things

Not long after I watched Haneke's film, a friend sent an e-mail in which he cited the William Carlos Williams poem "The Red Wheelbarrow,"[2] whose first two lines — "So much depends / upon" — serve as a prompt for each of the seventy-one fragments that constitute the essay. I first read Williams's poem in a book; to behold a truncated version of it in an electronic communication sparked a reverie about dependence and relativity.

C. Things Fall Apart

Maybe I am attracted to extant remnants because what remains — of people, literature, civilizations — is reconstructed from shards. Such "orts and fragments," as Virginia Woolf named them, have always mesmerized me. It's all anyone ever had of Sappho (to name one example), and it was enough — at least for me — because those scraps engender speculation (a key ingredient in the essay). Fragments, like gaps and white spaces, invite the reader to participate in the creation of a narrative. We learn this as children when we hear about Humpty Dumpty's great fall; while "all the king's horses and all the king's men / couldn't put Humpty together again," as listeners to the story, we reassemble the eggman and watch as he falls apart, over and over again.

Because I was playing with fragmentation and also with a call-and-

2. "The Red Wheelbarrow" is a prescient illustration of Williams's famous dictum that there are "no ideas but in things," an assessment that appears in his later epic work *Paterson* (which, along with Whitman's *Leaves of Grass*, is an essay disguised as a poem). First the poet shows us the red wheelbarrow, an object; simultaneously, he attends to the idea inherent in the thing upon which "so much depends"; and then quickly thereafter he wordpaints the image of it, "glazed with rain / water / beside the white / chickens." Through a single image, the reader is invited to imagine all that depends upon the singular beauty of the ordinary and to contemplate at the same time ideas evoked by a particular thing, including agriculture, weather, husbandry, and the relationship of people (who are absent in the poem/image but present by association) to nature.

response between writer and reader, I used only three lines of Williams's poem in the epigraph to the essay. I wanted readers to hear the lines (and to find/read the rest of the poem if they were unfamiliar with it) and/or to conjure for themselves a red wheelbarrow and discover in the thing and its image their own meanings.

Embedded in the essay are ideas and images distilled from the work of other writers (citation being one hallmark of the personal essay), all of whom are noted in the footnote at the bottom of the first page of my essay. In this way the essay is also a kind of puzzle (playfulness being another hallmark of the personal essay), which asks readers to find within it the references planted there and hints at the dialogue across space and time to which writing belongs. This essay, while not written in verse, also functions as a poem might, each fragment a stanza, or room, in which an idea and/or image resides.

III. Conclusion

The essay is a fluid form; it shapeshifts: were we living in a publishing marketplace or experiencing a literary consciousness that, respectively, truly valued and understood the essay, Haneke's film and Williams's poem might both be called essays, the former visual; the latter visualized, or, put another way, one filmic, the other in verse.

To *essay* is to attempt, to puzzle out, to look for the missing piece, to not necessarily find it, to carry on in putting back together what is looked for and maybe not found, to be the biographer of a thought or the cartographer of cognition, to associate things not normally associated. The essay's plot is contrived of mapping the synapses firing in the brain to produce idea. The speaker is called a narrator, who, when wearing a disguise, is called a persona. The essayist is the ultimate mad scientist, abandoning hypothesis and thesis to collect and distill a drop of consciousness. In the end, all we can do is try to assemble pieces of a story, and tell it, bit by bit.

Paul Maliszewski

Headaches

Pain, behind my eye. It's a kind of pushing, this pain, like something impossible is being insisted upon, some crude point in a long-running argument. This is my left eye.

The headache starts at the back of my head, somewhere toward the top, the part that sticks out a bit. But then the pain moves, shifting slowly forward, until it covers the whole top of my head.

It feels like somebody—somebody strong—is grabbing the back of my head and squeezing.

Another pain behind my eye. The right eye this time.

A new pain, this one larger than my head. It's a force, pressing down on me. The pain is larger than my head but still shaped like my head. It's like an electromagnetic cloud, hanging there, surrounding me. I forget what I do, if I do anything. It doesn't matter. I can't remove myself from the cloud.

The headache—this was another headache—did go away finally, though it lingered for hours, for the rest of the day, in fact. It was as if there were these little wisps of pain, souvenirs from a time when things were worse.

My wife can feel a bad headache coming on. She has to stop what she's doing and lie down in a dark room, or else the pain will get so bad, it won't go away. Last night, she felt one of those headaches. "I haven't had one of these in a while," she said.

"Can I get you anything?" I asked. "Some tea?"

"I don't think so," she said. She turned in the bed, away from the light.

"What about your sleep mask thing?" I said. My wife has a sleep mask she wears sometimes, to rest.

"That's cold," she said. "The cold will just constrict the blood vessels even more." She pulled the sheets up over her head and let them down on her face. "Do you know what a migraine is?" she asked.

I didn't, not exactly anyway.

She explained then about the blood vessels in the brain and the blood flowing through them.

"What's a regular headache?" I asked.

She wasn't sure.

"I could warm up the sleep mask," I said. "In some warm water." She said she'd like that, so I turned out the lights in the room and walked down the hall, turning out the lights as I went. Downstairs, I boiled some water for the sleep mask. While I waited, I sat at the bottom of the stairs and read some book just because it was handy.

I once went to sleep with a light headache. It was there, though easy enough to ignore. I thought it was on its way out, but when I woke up, I still had the headache. It might have been slightly worse.

Another headache today. I picture my brain wrapped, encircled, held fast by a thing with tentacles.

My wife said she once got a headache that lasted a month.

"A month?" I said. I thought I must have heard her wrong.

She went to several doctors, but they could do nothing to help her. They had no idea what was causing her headache. Finally, she went to one who gave her a shot.

"A shot of what?" I said.

She couldn't remember.

A few days later, my wife told me that she remembered something else: when she had the headache that wouldn't go away, she needed to have a CAT scan. We had been watching a movie in which a character got a CAT scan. It occurred to me that I had little idea what a CAT scan even is. Like with so much else, I just said the words, not knowing what they meant, what the procedure entails or what the scan might reveal. And yet I pictured something when I said the words. I saw a patient in a white room. I saw her lying down. I saw a machine moving over the patient, as if grazing on her. Or perhaps the machine was placed around her head. The machine shot rays. Emitted rays? The picture grew vague here.

The way a headache, when it's just starting to come on, makes me feel queasy from its power. As if I'm being yelled at from a close distance by someone I do not know. I'm in an elevator, I'm on a subway car, I'm now in the corner of a crowded room when a stranger notices me and approaches. I look away, thinking nothing, really—about meals, people from high school I haven't thought of in years, my half-formed plans for another day. The stranger, though, has an urgent message for me. "You will hurt next," he says. I could fold right there.

My wife writes. "I have a headache," she says. "I'm eating a very good cookie though."

The other night, at a department store, I felt a light pain at the back of my head. The pain had a roughly rectangular shape, as if someone were inserting his flattened hand, fingers first and palm down, into my head. It wasn't pleasant, but it wasn't excruciating either. It was just the inkling of a headache, an early warning, like bells pealing from towers in the village down the road. I told my wife, "I think I'm getting a headache. I'm gonna go get a Coke." She said she'd come with me. She had done what she wanted to do. We made our way through jewelry and purses and then makeup.

I was watering the plants when I got this pain on the top of my head. It was toward the back a little ways, maybe more to the left than the right. The pain was heavy, as if boards were stacked there, balancing on a point. For a few seconds, the pain flared up and then faded just as quickly. Some minutes went by, and I continued watering, but then the pain returned, in the same place, flaring up and then fading again.

I had been meaning to eat breakfast. I meant to make eggs. I meant to toast an English muffin and pour a tall glass of orange juice. I was thinking of just what sort of eggs to make. I was wondering if we had any jam. You must eat, I thought. No more thinking about eating.

I met my wife at her work and we walked to the Japanese place. I already had quite a headache coming on. The usual hunger pains in my face. There had been no food in the house for breakfast, and no time in the morning to grab even a glass of juice, as I had to teach early and, of course, was running late.

By the time we sat down with our food, I was in some pain, so rather than start eating, which could only have helped, I took off my glasses and squeezed the bridge of my nose and then rubbed my eyes for several seconds. The rubbing imprinted triangular bursts across the insides of my eyelids.

After lunch, I went to get my hair cut. My head was probably hurting just as much, if not more. A woman took me to the line of chairs and sinks to wash my hair. As she started to work the soap into my scalp, I had this sense—it was a distinct sense—that my headache was a knob attached to a post, and that her vigorous rubbing was liable to snap it off. The thought scared me at first, but then I wondered if that wasn't exactly what I needed, if in fact washing my hair or even just going through the motions was the cure I had been looking for. As it turned out, washing was no help. It only made me more aware of the pain. The woman toweled my hair dry, and I became so conscious then of my headache that I swore I felt it move, jarred inside my skull, as if it had come loose and I was just some container for pain. Later, the woman who cuts my hair took a comb to my head, and I thought, "She is combing my headache now."

At the National Gallery of Art, the guards are getting migraines from the new exhibition. It's the art that's doing it, that's causing the awful headaches. The works of art—the installations, whatever they call them—are made from long fluorescent tubes. Bright purples and greens and pinks arranged into geometric shapes, patterns. Walls lined with lights. The guards have taken to wearing sunglasses, but that doesn't seem to be enough.

Yesterday I had a headache for so long—a slight, pinching headache behind the bridge of my nose—that it became background to whatever I was thinking, just another part of my day, like scenery. The new normal.

I write my wife:

> Home now. House smells like tar. Someone a couple of doors down must be getting a new roof or something. I think they were working on it when we left. Still going. Smells bad. I need to eat, but I think this will give me a headache. How are you?

That headache I had is coming back. I can feel it getting stronger. I don't know what it's like. It's bad.

The belief, acquired from where, I'm not sure, that I should avoid taking aspirin if at all possible, that I should instead just be patient and try to relax, maybe massage my temples lightly or rub my eyelids. The belief that by relaxing, my headache will go away, just like that. The suspicion that maybe I take too much aspirin already, though how can that be? Surely there are people, many people, who take more aspirin much more often than I.

The time, years before, when I ground my teeth in my sleep and woke up with headaches. I was full-time at the newspaper and then full-time at the political report company plus I was teaching classes at night. Every morning my jaw was sore and my head hurt.

Last night I couldn't sleep, so I got up to read. A couple of hours later, I still didn't feel the least bit tired, but I thought I'd best try again to sleep. I was lying in bed, on my back, my left arm across my eyes, when I started to feel a headache coming on. Was it a hunger headache? I wondered. Had I not eaten enough? I'd skipped breakfast, but that wasn't anything new.

By the next day, in the afternoon, my headache had faded somewhat, but it hadn't exactly gone away. It was faint, like Muzak, something I became aware of only occasionally, when I concentrated, when I really listened for it. Ah, yes, there it is, still playing and still the same song.

The complaint, often voiced, that someone gives another person a headache. My clients, you'll hear, are giving me headaches. These students give me a headache. You're giving me a headache, my love.

The headache came, it seemed, out of nowhere. I was fine and then, when next I realized, I felt intense pressure, shaped like the palm of a hand, pressing at the back of my head, as if someone were trying to lift me up. At the same time I felt a sharp, pointed pain underneath my right eye. The two-pronged attack.

The pain in my head that made my teeth ache in sympathy. Then, later, the pain that felt so great, so enormous, that I felt like I was going to throw up.

A new pain has appeared at the back of my head. I thought it was a pressure, something pushing me away, but it feels instead as if I'm hanging, swinging from a string looped through two holes in the back of my skull. I rest my head and just try to massage it in the place where the string would attach, but I wonder if it's possible for me to rub such pain away. Isn't the whole point of massage that someone else exerts force, rubbing away one's pains, kneading one's knotted muscles? But the pain isn't just rubbed away, vanishing. The pain transfers. Someone rubs another's shoulders until his hands and fingers begin to cramp. To massage yourself, as I do my head, you have to exert your own force. In other words, one pains oneself just by trying to address the original pain, in this case, my headache. Seems fairly pointless, rubbing my head, when I think about it.

I awoke at 3:30 with a clamping pain at the back of my head. I lay in bed for several hours, until it was time to get up.

My father told me that my uncle, his brother, had headaches all the time. He worries, my father does. His brother died recently. Something to do with his brain. Not a hemorrhage. Not a lesion. I can't think of the word now. Tumor.

For the second day in a row, I woke up early with a great pain in my head, in the back, like a claw. It's often like a claw, I think. My wife said it's probably my sinuses. I have a cold of some sort. Or a flu. I never learned the difference.

A few hours later, the claw was back, clamping onto the same spot at the back of my head. I rubbed at it as if there was something there that I could loosen. This time the claw was lighter, fainter even. Compared to the claw I woke up to this morning, and the claw of the morning before, this grip felt almost fond. Like a firm handshake after a productive business meeting.

Another morning, another headache. Terrible pain, again at the back of my head. A gripping, yes, but also the feeling of being pushed from behind, as if someone were trying to press the back of my head into the front, collapsing it. Jesus.

After the pain, there remains the memory of the pain. A dim reminder in the same place, feeling the same as before, just less intense. I am relieved, like I've survived something but also like I've been released. At such moments, I wonder where the pain goes when it does finally go. Does the pain just disperse, or somehow disappear? Or is the pain still always there, existing as potential pain, the way a length of string can be said to contain the potential for many knots?

Had the start of a headache last night, the sensation of something forceful that had not yet arrived, something just in the vicinity, around the block maybe. My wife was talking to me, saying how she had ordered various items online, but all I could do was feel my head. She was getting ready to go to the gym, dressing, tying her shoes. I closed my eyes. I may have slept, but only for a few minutes. Whatever it was, it was enough. The next thing I knew, my wife was in the doorway, leaning, saying she was going now. "My head feels better," I said. "I don't know how, but it does."

Woke up this morning with that gripping pain at the back of my head. The claw again. Like something dug in there. I lay in bed for a while, for as long as I could, just rubbing at the back of my head, massaging it. Sometimes I think that helps a little.

Paul Maliszewski

On "Headaches"

Articulating the Inexplicable

On November 10, 2004, at a little after 4:00 p.m., I started keeping a journal, for lack of a better word, in which I tried to describe my headaches. I was getting headaches then that I thought of as odd. They felt different, the pains more articulated and baroque. I wanted to find a way to write about these pains. I wanted to capture in words how the headaches felt, the way they came on, and how they seemed to move over my head, ebbing, flowing, weakening, and then gathering power. I started to pay attention to them instead of attempting to ignore or forget them. When I got a headache, I added a bit to the journal. I also wanted to describe the headaches accurately and in a way that would be meaningful to someone else. Perhaps that's the challenge of all writing, to make the subjective meaningful, but when writing about headaches, I sometimes wondered if my descriptions even made sense on a literal level. Did the occasional metaphor bring added clarity, I wondered, or did it get in the way, like a cloud rolling over the true subject, obscuring it from view? Sometimes I wrote about my headaches while I was having them, the better to record the particular sensations.

I didn't imagine this would become an essay. For a while I thought maybe I'd use bits of the journal as raw material for some short story, my headaches transformed into just so much fictional detail, a problem for a character to bear. The more I added to the file, however, the more I started to wonder if, perhaps, the headaches could stand on their own somehow.

"Headaches," as I'd taken to calling the record of my pain, is unlike anything else I've written, whether story or essay. *Written* seems not quite the right verb for the work I've done here. I wrote the journal, of course, but to make this essay, I mostly excerpted and arranged select pieces from the original document. I was a cutter and a shaper more than a writer. I proceeded how I imagine a collagist works, seeing how pieces, if arranged just so, can form patterns, create implications, and generate meaning.

In its subject matter, "Headaches" remains a distant cousin to the few personal essays I've done. They're all personal, of course, but those other essays concerned observable realities larger than the cramped space inside my skull. They had characters in them, people who said and did things that I, in turn, could relate to readers. There were facts, too, in those essays, as well as details and data, all of which people could, if they wished, find in the world and confirm for themselves. I chose not to resort to experts to explain headaches. Certainly, one could write an essay about current research into the causes and treatment of headaches, but I didn't want a perspective outside of the headaches themselves and what they felt like. I wanted the essay to be limited, honestly, to what I know. Not what I could read up on and become seemingly conversant in, just what I know. That meant, too, preserving what I don't know, showing the places where my knowledge, such as it is, gives way to gaps, guesswork, and ignorance. I did, I suppose, end up cheating a little, by including accounts of my wife's headaches and a couple of e-mails and conversations we had about them. But when physical descriptions did not alone suffice, when metaphors conveyed only part of the experience, I turned, as I suppose was inevitable, to narrative.

Still, "Headaches" is—there's no getting around it—frighteningly solipsistic. It's self-involved by definition. And yet I—author and first-person narrator—don't make an appearance until the fifth section.

Mostly I appear in the background, a dim presence, a mere modifier—my head, my eye, my teeth. "Pain," the essay begins, "behind my eye." I might have started it, more straightforwardly, "I have a pain behind my eye," but I am not my real subject here. This is, finally, about the headaches.

Michael Martone

Asymmetry

I could actually close my eye. I had to
think about it. Think, "Blink!" to blink.
But it wasn't so much a blink. It was
more like weightlifting, locating the
muscle of the lid and then sustained
concentration, feeling as if I was
hauling down an overhead garage
door through muscled telepathy.
No, it was more hydraulic, the fluid
replaced by a fluid energy that I
forced, via my mind, to flow. The
lid slid down. Not so much a blink,
though, but an elaborately constructed
squint—a wreck of creased skin,
debris of lashes, twitching. I closed
my eye. I think I thought I couldn't
feel it. I had to go see it for myself.

I think there are a dozen cranial nerves.
VII is the facial nerve that provides the
underlying architecture of animation, of
expression. Two branches crisscross out
   of the brain, tickle the ears threading
beneath the lobe, and then fan into the
face to message the underlying muscle.
These nerves are not about transmitting
   feeling. Afflicted, I could still feel my
face and my face could feel. Hot, cold,
   pain, pleasure. No, the nerves there
   are about transmitting feeling, not to
   the brain, but broadcasting outward,
   staging muscle into the semaphore
      of expression, the wigwag of how
      we feel, not what we are feeling.

It is more than a little bit creepy to think
      of the entities that dwell in the nerve
   fabric that knits up our own thinking,
   the viruses latent there below, inside.
      Chicken pox nesting in the ganglia
      since the childhood infection and
   outbreak, cracking open and hauling
itself, hand-over-hand, along the strand
of the nerve to the skin there to express
   itself as shingles. Rashes, cold sores,
lesions. My face afflicted was featureless
   and smooth. Ironed, wrinkle-free. Not
the usual MO of a virus, the telltale trail
   of cell death. But, perhaps, they think,

a virus creeps, sleepwalks along the
sheath, makes it swell, fail. Antiviral
agents do nothing to the nothing that is
the palsy. A latent virus might short the
nerve or, for all they think, it might not.

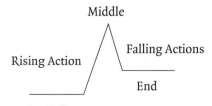

The famous map of narrative is
cockeyed. It's not the isosceles triangle
we imagine we imagine. The beginning,
middle, and end. Like the heft of letters
in the phrase "beginning, middle,
and end," narrative is asymmetrical,
skewed, shrinking as it expands after
the spike, a sloping away. The sighing
dénouement. Not a mountain in cross
section as much as the gesture of a drift,
the sheer face of the cliff all eroded
on the lee side of the climax. The
upside-down checkmark trails off . . .

It started with a smacking of my lips.
I smacked my lips. I have a bowl of
yogurt at night, most every night, a
dessert, watching *The Daily Show*. I use
a spoon, an old Northwest Airlines

flatware spoon. And that night spooning the yogurt into my mouth, squeegeed off the spoon by my lips, I half-heard the smack. I couldn't have made the sound. Odd, I half-thought.

Bell's palsy is diagnosed by excluding other causes the paralysis mimics—tumors, diabetes, Lyme disease, asymptomatic herpes zoster, head trauma, stroke, especially stroke. Stroke because it shares with Bell's the rapidity of the attack and its handedness. But in the differential, a stroke blacks-out a sizeable side of the body's real estate while Bell's blanks only one side of the face. Bell's is, then, what it's not. Idiopathic. Cryptogenic.

That night, I brushed my teeth. I tried to spit in the sink. The spit, instead of streaming toward the drain, vectored to the right and welled on the left, leaking out there in that corner of my mouth. Spitting, I had never given it a second thought. It seemed to be something one just does effortlessly, unconsciously until one is made conscious of it. I brush with my right hand. My hair is parted on the left. I don't look in the mirror as I brush my teeth but look

down into the ovoid stainless bowl. I
put the brush down, turned the right
(facing me) handle "on." Cold water.
And cupped my right hand to catch
a palm full of water, already spilling
out of my hand, and brought it to my
mouth. My ability to create suction was
off too, much of the water fell back
to the sink, the rest sloshing right,
seeping already as I leaned back down
to spit. I couldn't purse my lips. A fan
of spit with elevated levels of undiluted
toothpaste pasted the high, drier sides
of the bowl. Odd, I thought again.

Dr. Sally Bell Beck sat me down and told
me I was not insane. This was years ago.
I was a freshman at Butler University,
taking her introduction to psychology
class. She told me she had this talk with
many freshmen who, upon learning that
one definition of madness was for the
one who is mad not to know one is mad,
thought oneself mad. You are not mad,
she said, wiping at her right eye. But how
can I tell, I asked her, if the symptom of
my madness is that I don't know I am
mad. Dr. Sally Bell Beck sighed, gave me
her famous fish-eye stare. The right half
of her face, the sinister side facing her,
was frozen. The skin there pulled taut,

ironed. She was afflicted with some kind of permanent palsy that must have been with her since she was a student in college. In class, I would close my right eye, hold the textbook up to mask her face in half in class as she lectured, blotting out the still-animated side. The half that didn't move appeared to be that of a youth, an ingénue, airbrushed. She talked out of the other side of her mouth, a kind of pirate's bark. And she always carried a massive handkerchief to dab at her walleye. To blink, she rolled her head down, tucking her chin to her chest, every minute or so. Then she rolled her staring eye up under the passive lid. It reappeared, glossy, as her head rolled back up, pointing her chin to the ceiling. The tears that collected and spilled onto that smooth cheek she would dab away with the handkerchief.

The lecture she gave each year on the psychology of love was famous at the school and was always attended by former students, staff, and faculty. Each fall, word got around campus that this was the week for the love lecture. I went years after I was her student, crowded into the classroom where most of the auditors stood staring at Dr. Sally Bell Beck nodding and tearing as she talked.

"Crocodile tears" are thought to be synthetic sympathy, manufactured grief. The nerve now off-line producing the Bell's palsy in the muscles of my face also worms its way into the anterior two-thirds of my tongue. I was warned that, as the nerve rebooted, I might find myself crying at the taste and/or smell of food, a syndrome of crocodile tears. I might also salivate when I cried, but though the crossed wiring had a certain symmetry, the latter manifestation would be less noticeable, a minor key, distracted as I would be by the true sadness generating the authentic tears.

I enjoy the television series *House*. I watch the detective diagnostician drama in reruns while eating yogurt. I might have even been watching *House* the night the palsy struck. At my doctor's, I laughed, finding out that the measurement of my paralysis would be determined by the House Brackman Facial Nerve Grading System. The laugh spilled out of one side of my malfunctioning mouth, a characteristic of grade IV, moderately severe, function. I smiled my broken smile. It tickled as he measured "the lateral movement of the oral commissure."

I didn't think twice about the anomalies of the night before. The smacking of lips. The spraying of spit. The next day I held conferences all day in the student center. I staked out a table near the Starbucks concession where I can purchase an Izzi tangerine-flavored soda in a bottle I will nurse through the dozen half-hour meetings with students. I sat across the table from one, looking into his or her face as we talked, a kind of mirror, about rising action and falling action, the nature of fact and fiction, the depth and surface of character. As the day wore on I felt stranger and stranger. I noticed while drinking from the pop bottle that I couldn't form a seal around the opening. I could feel a weakness in my face growing weaker. I began to touch my face, knead the skin. It felt a little like a dentist's block, like it should be numb and with a phantom puffiness as if severely swollen. But when I actually touched my lips, they felt normal, and, even more strangely, I could feel, via my lips, my fingers touching there. I wasn't anesthetized, yet I wasn't all there.

Had the attack been worse and I had lost the ability to blink my left eye, I would have been prescribed an eye patch to protect it, to keep it from drying out. Instead, I seemed to weep, the tears welling out of my eye and running down my cheek.

With effort I could close my eye, blink away the tears. The attack had come on overnight and disappeared as quickly three weeks later. No eye patch. But no more wearing of contact lenses in order to avoid scratching the dehydrated cornea. The doctor had prescribed drops, artificial tears, to be administered before sleep just in case.

Lying down, I stared up toward the dropper, saw a drop suspended there, saw it fall, saw it accelerate toward my eye. My brain sent signals, I know.

Automatic messages were posted to protect the eye, but the lid didn't budge. The artificial tears splashed on my eye, the unblinking eye. There was a chance I slept then with one eye open. But after the drop I shimmied the eyelid closed through a concentrated effort. And once it was closed it stayed closed. It would be too hard to open. It patched itself. It stayed closed until the elaborate effort I had to muster the next morning to prop the lid open again.

At first I thought it was the right side
of my face that had gone haywire,
when it had been the left. The doctor
was on the phone. I had called him
from the conferences in the student
center. He asked which side of my face
was affected. I had the phone pressed
against my right ear. The right, I said.

I had just forced myself to smile.
The right side of the face snapped to
attention, the smile wedging the cheek
into the hand clutching the phone. The
right, I said. But, I think now, I thought
it was the right initially because the
movement there felt unnatural, the test
gesture was self-conscious, and, in the
absence of the other half of the face,
the sneering fragment of smile seemed
twitchy, a spasm, out of my control. In
contrast, the deadpan left side seemed
polite and understated in its demeanor,
seemed cautiously detached from

what felt like a manic neighbor, all slapstick and pratfalls, demonstrating its dexterity, its benign innervation.

Tying ties in the mirror. Ties untied are asymmetrical. The wide and the narrow. The long end and the short end draped around the neck, worked to the suitable off-balanced, out-of-kilter starting position. As I knotted my ties, I would mug into the mirror exaggerated grimaces, leers, sneers. Mined, mimed my mien. I aped aspect. But still half my face was dumb to the body language bouncing off the mirror. I couldn't raise a reaction in half of me that couldn't act. It was as if I was looking askance at my own death mask, that masquerade. The stalled side of my face was lifelike, waxy, true to life but lifeless. Affectless. Bored. There it was in deep in the depth of the mirror, elsewhere.

Let's get the stroke business out of the way right now. Talking to the doctor on the phone from the conference table in the coffee shop, I asked if this was a stroke. Could I move my arms? Could I hear? See? Were my legs numb? Could I speak? Yes, I said, yes to all of that. Except my legs. My legs weren't numb. Or, more exactly, hissed. I lisped though the bilabial consonants. I lost the b sound and the p. The lips on the one side of the face had opted out of the phonics, had sent in a kind of nasally inflected m, a mushy plosive, the air let out of the tire, a flat b. The lips on the port side had been mashed, felt swelled. Not a stroke with its serious erasures. This something else with its awkward muscle amnesia. Its bumbled mumbling. This profiled scourge. This vacant duplex, gone-fishing face.

Soon after the paralysis settled in, I took my doughy face to a student reading. I was still getting used to my condition. Should I drink from the bottle of water picked up from the refreshment table? Teaching, I am on the side that believes that the best strategy is to call attention to an anomaly before the students notice, get ahead of the distraction. Look, I cut myself shaving, I will say. Yes, I have a pimple on my nose. It is a meager attempt to take control of a situation out of your control. You provide a narrative. I meant for this mistake to happen. Look, I said at the reading, see anything different? The students gathered around the table, stared at me, at my face. I then launched a smile that morphed instantly into a leer, the droopy side of my face drooping as the muscled side flexed. My students effortlessly generated recognizable expressions of surprise, concern, puzzlement, even shock. I told them it was Bell's palsy. I have Bell's palsy. And rehearsed for them the sudden onset, the diagnosis, its duration. A few then related stories of their own or their family member's palsies in the past, attempting to re-create the uncanny sensation of sensing through absence, being made conscious of the unconscious world that usually envelopes us. A meta-discussion for a meta-face. We thought, my students said, you looked different. You looked, they said, more tired. During the readings, I did slump in my chair. A week into the event I was weakened by being weakened this way. A reading is not quite theater, a stepchild of a platform. I listened to poetry and prose, reacting to the words with delight and sadness. I was conscious of the masks masking my face, my faces.

I posted my face on Facebook. I was
fishing for comments. I took the picture
staring into the iMac's screen camera
in my office at home. The afflicted half
of my face is catching light from the
window that flattens it. That side is
flattened further by the contrast with the
rumpled topography of the other side,
all valleys and peaks. Comments began
to be posted. They were mini-memoirs
mostly, mapping the commentator's
own bout with the palsy. It was how we
take these little things for granted until
. . . The curl of a lip. The unconscious
blink. The eyebrow arch of surprise.
The scowl. The lost repertoire of our
character, characters. Coming face to
face with this stranger under the skin.

Michael Martone

On "Asymmetry"

The Typewriter Is Not a Typewriter

I always found it funny that, as writers, we use these incredibly powerful, twenty-first-century typesetting machines like mechanical typewriters of the nineteenth century.

The conventions of composition—leading, spacing, font type and size, margins, and borders—have essentially remained unchanged even as the technology of production has advanced exponentially. When I began to write in the 1970s—yes, I am that ancient—I used a typewriter, a Smith-Corona portable, to prepare a typescript for an editor to consider for publication and, if it was accepted, to then be used by the typesetter to prepare for printing. Many of the conventions of writing then (underlining a title of a book, say) were employed really as coded signals to the typesetter—<u>set this in italic type</u>—who controlled elements of composition only then available to the typesetter.

Today, with my powerful word processing software—mine, here, no different from the one used by most of my publishers to make finished books or magazines—I can indeed italicize my type myself as opposed to simply underlining it. It is effortless to do so.

But many fossil limitations of the mechanical typewriter survive, remain wired into us. Do you space once or twice after this question mark? The keyboard itself is vestigial. Its QWERTY make-up made purposefully difficult in order to hobble the keyboardist so as to slow the fingers of the typist and not jam the slow-reacting mechanical keys. The computer itself seems to want to mimic the typewriter. Programmed into the word processor software's default settings are precedents left over from the mechanical age in the choice of paragraph settings and indentations, justified left and ragged right margins, and so on.

It is incredibly difficult to imagine the graphic layout of a page of text—when being produced by a writer—in any other manner save this one inherited from the typewritten era. To this day writers unconsciously adhere to the normal, standard settings and acquiesce to their role as writers who produce only a text as text and allow others to handle the printing and graphic design elements.

This convention of graphic prohibition is reinforced by shared theoretical prescriptions that prevent a writer from straying out of line. The belief that a writer should create a "transparent" text, a text that does not call attention to itself as artifice, is deeply ingrained. Letters and words should be deployed only as abstract mental triggers to the concrete image and should not be used illustratively. Even the use of punctuation—the exclamation mark especially!—is considered too graphic, and the exclamation it produces, if it produces it at all, is considered synthetic, sentimental, inauthentic, and, oddly, as a kind of "showing" that is more like "telling."

So, even though as writers we have an array of graphic options at our fingertips we are prevented from using them. **No!** bold type! **No!** bold type that is underlined! **NO!** bold type that is underlined and set in all caps to reinforce and redundantly emphasize the emotion! Such flourishes are thought to be, at most, a cheap trick and therefore not to be trusted.

This particular set of proscriptions appears to be inviolate. To actually dabble in graphic particulars is to portray oneself as a rank amateur writer, innocent of the very basic and eternal rules of writing. One must prepare one's typescript in the traditional manner and not rely naively on "pictures" instead of words.

As the technology I use as a writer to write evolves and as the traditional venues in which I publish transform, I find it imperative to question, at least, these strictures and stints placed on me in the physical preparation and material nature of the prose I produce. A writer writes, but as a writer I find, more and more, that I am meant to take up the tasks of typesetting, editing, and, yes, even publishing. The powerful nature of the machines I now use—the computer and the Internet—redefines not only what a writer is and does but, even more essentially, who I am and what I do.

Ander Monson

Outline toward a Theory of
the Mine versus the Mind
and the Harvard Outline

I. Start with the Roman numeral I with an authoritative period
trailing just after it. This is the Harvard Outline, which comes in
Caps and is a method of organizing information
 a. remembered from high school as a major step toward
  creating an essay
   i. though there was a decimal method, too
 b. but I've never been comfortable with the thing—its seeming
  rigor, its scaffolding so white against the language
   i. never felt the top-down structuralist method of
    constructing writing to be useful or effective; the mind,
    so idiosyncratic, unusual
     1. its strangeness and its often-incoherence
      a. the lovely anomaly
 c. and the Harvard Outline is the reason that I get 55
  5-paragraph essays every month
 d. it is, I think, suspect, (its
 e. headings
   i. subheadings
    1. sub-subheadings
     a. etc.
     b. though there is a pleasure to this iteration,
      this recursion—like mathematics and the

algorithms I played with and admired in computer-science classes, writing functions that called themselves

    i. which called themselves

        1. which called themselves

            a. until they were satisfied

        2. and exited

    ii. right back

  c. out

    i. like those Russian nesting [*matryoshka*] dolls; a lovely symmetry; such satisfaction comes in nesting

    ii. such starkness

        1. elegance)

f. all those steps out and down across the page—like the writing task is that of going downhill, like a waterfall in its rush

    i. or the incremental, slow plod down the slope, skis buried behind in some drift

g. While technically called "the Harvard Outline"

    i. it has nothing to do with Harvard

        1. according to their archivists, "it appears to be a generic term"

    ii. so it's difficult to track it down in the history of organizing information

        1. which is what this culture spends increasing time (and money!) doing

            a. witness the amazing success of the search engine Google

                i. as created by Larry Page and Sergey Brin

                ii. with its elegant mechanism of concordance

1. of ranking searches by the number of
pages that link to each individual page
or site in order to establish the relative
importance of that initial page or site
   a. and look—there's no need for
   parentheses in 1. above thanks to
   the Harvard Outline
   b. again that attraction to self-
   examination
   c. again that attraction to what
   elegance there is to find

II. My family has a background in the Michigan mining industry
   a. a history in copper, iron, the cast-off leftover materials
   necessary to process ore from rock
   b. though less my recent family
      i. not my father who is a professor—whose job, like
      mine, is (reductively) the mining and refining, then the
      distribution of information for (small sums of) money
         1. though perhaps this is a cynical view of the profession
            a. and light-as-knowledge metaphor is hardly
            breaking new ground
         2. still I like the image of the light-helmeted professor
         plowing through the darkness
            a. though it is romantic to say the least
         3. "like mine" (from above)—mining is a story of
         possession
            a. of legal ownership of land and rights, the
            permission to go below the crust
         4. "breaking new ground" (from above)—again the
         construction terminology

       a. the invocation of the building, of the
          engineering
  5. my father teaches at Michigan Technological
     University, formerly the Michigan College of
     Mines, a school that is just about to lose its Mining
     Engineering program
       a. which is older than the oldest living humans
       b. which is "one of only 15 mining engineering
          programs in the U.S. that has been
          uninterrupted since the beginning of the
          century and has also held accreditation with
          the Accreditation Board for Engineering and
          Technology (ABET) since 1936" according to
          the MTU Mining Engineering website
            i. this tidbit brought to you by Google
           ii. this tidbit being no longer accurate (now
              we should use past tense, as the program
              has been retired, killed, phased out): this is
              an information shift between the writing of
              the essay and its publication
c. but further back
  i. since nearly everyone who emigrated to Upper Michigan
   from (mostly) Scandinavia worked in the mines, or
   worked in industries that supported it
     1. the mining boom in the 19th century was so big that
       Calumet, Michigan, population of 879 as of the 2000
       census, was nearly named the capitol of Michigan
     2. and there are stories of exploitation and immense
       hardship
       a. as there always are
     3. though just after WWII, the price of copper declined

and so—though there's still plenty underneath the
northern earth—the mines slowly shut their doors

    a. now there are no active producing mines left in
       the Keweenaw

         i. the railroads no longer run

        ii. even the Greyhound bus service has
           stopped

       iii. it felt at times while growing up like living
          in a dead-letter office

           1. another information shift: evidently
              there are still two mines that remain
              in operation, one of which my high
              school friend Jeremy, his father a
              metallurgist, is working for

    b. though the shells they left behind—the
       fine network of tunnels that still riddle the
       earth—are havens for millions of bats

         i. who come out at night through the chicken
          wire that often covers up the mines' mouths

        ii. and were—until recently, when the method
          of closing off the mines was changed to
          be a bit more bat-friendly—picked off by
          hundreds of raccoons that would sit at the
          chicken wire, waiting for the daily exodus
          and feast

    c. and now Upper Michigan is a destination for
       bat-watching tourists

  d. and anyone growing up in the Keweenaw has had ready
    access to mines

       i. either through the tours of the few remaining open
         tourist mines

1. which are absolutely worth doing, though expensive (to the tune of $25), because to be submerged a mile underneath the earth is a necessary experience
   a. to get that absolute darkness
      i. even if you think you know what it's like
   b. and to get that absolute chill
   c. to know what your ancestors went through
      i. or at least to have an idea—isn't this an honor or an obligation?
ii. or more likely illegally
   1. breaking the locks off the doors
      a. because there are hundreds of old shafts sunk in the land that haven't been filled
   2. drinking inside (also arguably a family obligation), or exploring with rope, flashlights, and a constant sense of possibility
      a. for there is something beautiful, nearly unbearable, about a hole in the earth
         i. about darkness
            1. that unknown
               a. black box
                  i. big X
         ii. maybe it's a male fixation
      b. that it must bear exploration, no matter how far down it goes
         i. maybe it's too many Hardy Boys books, or Jules Verne
      c. and also there's the danger
         i. a definite attraction
            1. one cure for boredom
            2. a cheapie dangerous carnival ride

iii. or possibly through the few research mines maintained by the University

   1. one of which I discovered while hiking in Hancock, Michigan

      a. while it's not a public mine, it is not gated or barred off

      b. walk within a quarter of a mile and you'll feel the drop in temperature caused by the cool air streaming out

         i. a counterintuitive finding—remember high school geology, the earth's crust, mantle, core, etc., and lava bursting out through craters

         ii. or Jules Verne again

            1. while less than absolutely reliable

         iii. and how it gets hotter now

            1. the further

               a. in

                  i. you go

         iv. how there's a pressure from the outside structure

            1. how the structure

               a. either binds you in or wants to expel you like a sickness

               b. think the mine, the outline, as a body

               c. an ecosystem

               d. or a mechanical spring

                  i. compress

                  ii. release

                  iii. repeat

> v. and that structure creates pressure; how
> architecture is the elegant distribution of
> stress

III. The outline, so like a mine
   a. defined by penetration
      i. deeper in
      ii. both laterally and vertically
         1. for harder information
      iii. yes, how male, again, you dirty bird
   b. and mining is interested mostly in the horizontal
      i. mineral deposits—in the absence of fault or other
        geologic strangeness—lay naturally in planes
      ii. since similar materials respond similarly to pressure,
        they settle horizontally
      iii. and the goal of the miner is to identify the deposit
         1. in terms of *dip and strike*
            a. the straight line of maximum inclination (*dip*)
            b. the horizontal line, the contour line (*strike*)
   c. and the vertical when necessary, to either follow the vein
      i. or to proceed deeper into the earth once the vein has
        been exhausted
   d. though the terminology of the mine is far more lovely than of
   the outline
      i. *level, incline, drifts, shaft, crosscut, winze, raise* and *mouth* and
        face, gossan, apex, shaft, adit, gangue, stope
      ii. *"Shallow Boring in Soft Rocks: Boring by Hand Auger"*
         1. chapter subheading from the "Boring" chapter,
          Introduction to Mining by Bohuslav Stočes
      iii. having an essential mystery to them
         1. due to their inaccessibility

      a. compare to that of the Harvard Outline, designed particularly (one imagines — though it's not clear who designed it) to be easily negotiable

  2. and the aura of danger, of esoteric, academic, secret knowledge about them

      a. they literally describe loci of danger, pits and sinkholes; they offer both treasure and death

          i. both of which have a lure

iv. and I was obsessed with mining for the first 10 years of my life

  1. visiting the A. E. Seaman Mineralogical Museum at Michigan Technological University

      a. which has the 17-ton copper boulder, the largest mineral specimen ever taken from Lake Superior

      b. an emblem of the Keweenaw, one of the world's richest copper deposits

  2. trying to convince my dad to buy me various geological supplies

      a. such as the rock tumbler I never really used — a sad emblem of my childhood sitting on a shelf maybe in my parents' basement

  3. agate hunting along the shores of Lake Superior

  4. looking for chunks of unrefined copper in the woods or in the hills of stampsand along Portage Canal (the canal that cuts off the tip of the Keweenaw Peninsula from Michigan)

      a. leftovers from processing iron ore

      b. which very well may be poisoning some Michigan lakes

    i. and we try not to think too much about this
5. making homemade explosives according to the
   often-poor instructions from Paladin Press books
   and other, even less reliable sources
      a. ceasing only when a good friend of mine lost 3
         fingers
v. and in a way, I still am—as it's the central story of the
   place where I am from, the big goodness and the tragedy
   1. it is how I imagine the ghost of slavery is to Southern
      writers
         a. having this central, public history contributes
            to there even being such a thing as a "Southern
            Writer," whereas there aren't as obviously
            "Northern Writers"
   2. (the boom and the bust—the makings of story
      itself)
         a. and certainly the makings of much of my family
e. perhaps it's only my desire
   i. that this, my kind of work
      1. darkness on light onscreen, then on the page
   ii. be worth as much as what my family did in the dark for
       hours, for days, for years
f. and the metaphor of mining one's past or childhood for
   writing material
   i. an apt construction, experience as *material*
   ii. is used a lot, and is something I'm concerned about
       myself
      1. the ethics and the economics of the writing act
         a. and that other pressure that it entails
            i. so maybe the outline is a kind of
               architecture I am trying to erect

  ii. to protect myself against my family,
   meaninglessness, and the future
    1. an artifice to get inside the past
    2. like a cold and unlit hole—what family
     tragedy is there behind me glittering
     like a vein
  iii. perhaps it is a womb
    1. and this then has to do with my
     mother's death
    2. a protective sheath, a comfort zone
  iv. or it could be a shell
 b. an attempt for rigor as some buffer or
  protection
 c. or maybe it is elegance for the sake of it
 d. an infinite recursion
 e. some wankery
2. then there's always the possibility of being stuck,
 candle snuffed by a sudden blast
 a. the candles that my family would have to buy
  themselves and carry—lit—down into the earth,
  the candles that were the only protection against
  the emptiness and isolation
 3. with no way of lighting up again, and no way
iii. back out—

Ander Monson

Outline toward a Reflection on the Outline and the Splitting of the Atom, I Mean the Colorado River, I Mean Our Collective Attentions, or Maybe I Mean the Brain, Which Is Mostly Forks, You Know

I. I'm not sure that I can claim that this essay stretches the boundaries of what the essay can do

   a. for starters, the whole point of the essay for me is that it is without boundary, plastic, massive, sprawling, starlike, less about product or any specific shape or form than about the process of finding its own form, its own subject

      i. though I do like thinking of myself as a boundary pusher

         1. *see also* my hacker past

            a. which I really need to stop referencing, because it's getting old by now

               i. by which I mean I'm getting old by now

                  1. see also my receding hairline

                  2. my lust for the young

                  3. my general sense of foolishness

                     a. and decay

         2. *see also* my difficulty with reverence

         3. *see also* my love for reference

         4. *see also* my often-obsessive experiences in video

games or other simulated worlds as I move along the
outside of the area designated for exploration, trying
to find the boundaries

    a. *there are always boundaries*

        i. *always edges of these created spaces*

            1. *always something there to keep me from
infinity*

                a. *see also* "Essay as Hack" on my
website

                    i. <otherelectricities.com>

b. and that plasticity of form, a seeming endlessness, is what
attracts me to most writing, in particular the essay, which is
as close to a (simulated, I admit—pruned and trimmed and
spliced and *worked*) wander that you can get. I'd say meander,
the natural action of boundaryless water, as Mary Paumier
Jones explains in her short essay "Meander" in *Creative
Nonfiction* from a ways back, but that risks encapsulating my
own name in the essential action of the genre that I've come
to love, and that feels somehow incidentally (or not) wack, so
I'm not doing so here

    i. note that I appear to be having it both ways (in fact doing
so here, and saying I'm not); that's a character flaw too

        1. or maybe less flaw than feature

            a. this is perhaps for the future to decide

                i. or the reader

                    1. so go to it, yo!

    ii. and in a way the essay gets to have it both ways

        1. we think and act;

        2. we think and think and rethink and act;

        3. we leave traces of our former rivulets on the desert
floor

a. that anyone can see for a while—that brain
doing its brainsprawl thing on the page
　i. though sometimes what it does is not
　appealing or meaningful or wonderful, and
　thereby needs to be rained back in
　　1. I mean reined, but the water
　　metaphors start to overspill the brain's
　　capacity to keep it straight
　　　a. this is in fact one of the errors that
　　　I try to build into my generative
　　　states when the brain moves faster
　　　than the hands, so that I type the
　　　wrong thing, but instead of editing
　　　it out, I leave it in for now, wanting
　　　to trust my errors, chaos traces,
　　　some evidence of the brain doing
　　　something else below intention
　　　　i. I come back to them in
　　　　revision to decide which bits
　　　　connect or spark or mean,
　　　　and which do not, and if I felt
　　　　this one did not it would have
　　　　been edited out, which it has
　　　　not, at least thus far
　　　　ii. (is this essay done? is the printed
　　　　essay ever done? is brainwork
　　　　ever done? can it be fixed? and is
　　　　it okay to say if not?)
4. so they're there—still visible—just history now;
history that hopefully is readable or interesting to
someone sometime (maybe you)

II. I believe the essay (and when I say essay I mean brain, or maybe vein that leads to or from the brain) is more waterform than anything, that it will fill up to any boundary, any channel, man-made or not, and if it finds that channel insufficient for its flow and bulk and speed and action, then it will find a new channel or make a new channel, and we'd be best advised to let it do its thing

    a. not to suggest that it needs no coaching, no teasing, no crimping or clamping, no nudging, no motion control running shoes to stop the body from doing what it wilt what it shalt (will it ever wilt?) (I think it will eventually)

        i. in this way it is like thought

            1. which as any neurotic (or writer, or insomniac, or sometimes all three in one body) will tell you will spill over into whatever space you leave aside for it

                a. that is unless you control it with drugs or therapy or thinking or physical exhaustion

                    i. like running

                    ii. like sex

                    iii. like calisthenics

                        1. or like all three consecutively, or not in that order

            2. so that you find your nights consumed with the overspill of the unconscious and uncontrollable into the conscious or barely conscious brain, thus starting that sickly spinning motion that we know we're in trouble when it begins

    b. I've been thinking a lot about waterforms lately (and sometimes late at night—I am only barely avoiding an unfortunate reference to a particularly meaningless Billy Joel song in this moment; said implied reference might or might not be edited out later—is it better to show my work, like on tests for partial credit, or better to hide and try to simulate some magic?)

    i. in this way I was thinking a lot about thinking and about mines and material metaphors and where they come from before I wrote this essay

        1. and in part the essay was the outcome of that question about the "Harvard Outline" and what it was, where it came from, whether it was connected with Harvard University

        2. in another part it was a hack, an idea that this form might be fun to play with, to see what it could do

            a. because it was so regimented

                i. so restricted

                ii. so restrictive

                iii. so restorative, that form, those rules

        3. and in other ways you should absolutely not trust what any writer has to say about their writing, and certainly not me, since I am human too, prone to self-aggrandizement, neurosis, fumbling, a convenient forgetting impulse, self-mythologizing, past-tense revision, belief in bad ideas, etc.

            a. so in this way I have no idea where the essay came from, or what it challenges (aside from the obvious formal constraints of the outline form which are pretty obvious), or where it goes, or what subconscious strata gave rise to it

                i. and the more important thing then is that I found some action, some magic, some excitement there in the form and the way in which it processed and shaped the content

                    1. though to be clear I don't believe in the

separation of form from content: and
certainly not in an essay like this that's
so overtly formal that you can't help but
be aware of that foregrounding of form

a. which makes for a double reading
experience, right? you know it's
an outline, and you know it's an
essay, and you know it's kind of
neither, but somehow it's both,
like a transformer, like, you know,
more than meets the eye, like
robots in disguise, like the way
in which any of our individual or
collective childhood obsessions
might have given rise to any
intellectual spark that might take
a dozen years, or twenty, or fifty,
to come to fruition

i. this is what I've learned
about the brain and age
and apparent (or real)
randomness, that there are
slow processes and fast ones,
and we are almost never even
close to aware of any of the
processes or their durations
and half-lives running at any
time in this thing that we have
to reckon with on the page,
every night after everyone else
has gone to bed and we're

awake, insomniac, unsatisfied
with our thinking and the
shapes it makes

    b. so that binary—form and
content—is bogus on a deep level
for me as a thinker and writer,
even as it's so useful in finding
ways to talk about art that it is
impossible to dispose of in any
substantive and permanent way

  ii. and isn't the result

    1. that tracking of the process on the page

      a. frozen, cold, static

      b. though once it was obviously
pretty hot and brain-electric and
all sinuous and subconscious

  iii. what matters most?

  iv. I think it does.

    1. and then I think, hey, bogus, isn't the
result a process too? Yes, I think, it's
also that, but product too—and that's
the trick to art: it's both when it's any
good at all

  v. And you can see, I hope, my re-engagement
in the form in this articulation of what I
have in mind by form and content, essayist
and essay, brain and page and space

ii. partly as a corollary to my recent thinking about
waterforms and rivers now

  1. and how one line of thinking might suggest both
forms is maybe worth a brief stopover

2. since though the outline essay suggests the stratification, the ranking of points and logical argument, in some ways the mine that I'm arguing for as well as an exploratory instinct
3. the mine is also a space to be filled
4. as the essay is a space to be filled
5. as the mine is also composed of what's removed—space not solid
   a. yet the mine is not the mine tailings or the ore or the stampsand and what's been taken out and processed
   b. the mine is process, is form, is in a way equivalent to the very act of mining
   c. in the way the river is not the water that flows through the river but the space through which it flows somehow conflated with the water
      i. this is in some ways notes toward another essay I'm working on at the moment about water, but I'm going to let that waterthink invade this space because that's what water does, especially when confronted with a mine, a space, a hollow channel leading somewhere
      ii. so that a river dry for most of the year (like Tucson's Rillito River) is still considered a river
         1. on account of the massive flow that fills its bed due to snowmelt or monsoon season
         2. no one witnessing this flow (16,000 cubic feet per second by some

measurements) would confuse this
river with an empty space

    d. so the outline is not just form and not just
content but some molten fuse of the two—it is
process and constraint

    e. that is, if I'm doing it right, if it's a two-way
pressure system so that both are primary and
secondary in their turns, so that both exert
pressure on the other, and both must coexist or
fail, like dikes, like floodplain walls

6. so you can see the metaphor lined up: the essay
too is something to be filled—with intention,
maybe, with our own thinkings, because in the
essaying we hope to stumble on what it is we think
through experiment and repetition, through the
juxtaposition of lines of inquiry we might have once
thought interesting enough to jot down on the white
space of the page and in so doing enshrine them as
ours

III. so even this essay's form has been filled up again (and has filled
itself again) appropriately, unstoppably

    a. at least not by me

        i. and who would want to stop it?

        ii. and who could stop it?

        iii. and who is brazen enough to think that they could tame
water into submission?

           1. I mean besides civil engineers and the builders of
hydroelectric dams and hydrogeologists, and sailors
since time immemorial

               a. who mostly died, right?

      i. opening up the mass space of myth, decade after decade
         1. the mass space of literature
         2. a sea of seas
         3. unknown beyond unknown
         4. so that we find a name for it again
         5. with every encounter?

2. I mean besides most of those who've settled the American West with its dearth of water

3. I mean besides the engineers who split and split and split the Colorado into trickles

4. I mean besides the fools like myself who live and love in Tucson (recent recipient of a portion of the Colorado River water via the Central Arizona Project) and mind their water usage, knowing where it comes from

    a. without whom there would be no West, no smug sense of postcollege liberal environmental guilt
      i. dickweeds!
      ii. friends!
    b. and without whom perhaps there is no solution nor exigency to find one or articulate the pressures on our settlements and civilizations

5. I mean besides readers of essays who blow through essays like water, who drink art, who are nourished by its tributaries and its splittings and resplittings so even the smallest bit might find something living and bring it out into the world

    a. which I hope this thing does
      i. he says grandiosely
         1. but not without some sense of hope

Dinty W. Moore

Four Essential Tips for Telling the Truth in Personal Memoir and Securing That Blockbuster Book Deal

With Helpful Writing Prompts and Exercises!!

You want to be a writer but find yourself repeatedly stumped by the difference between fact and fiction? Well hey, Buster, who wouldn't be? Fact and fiction both begin with the letter *f*, after all, and they share a *c* and a *t*.

Confusing stuff!

Moreover, knowing the difference between what really happened to you a few years back and what you imagined only yesterday is a daunting challenge. I mean, do they expect us to remain sober twenty-four seven?

There was that worthless sap—James *Something*—who was sure that he had languished in a federal lockup for ten years or so, enjoying baked ziti dinners with notorious Italian mobsters. He wrote that bestselling book about it. *A Million Little Pizzas?* Turns out, though, the guy only spent five hours in a small-town Ohio police station.

Easy mistake. Could have happened to anyone.

But I digress. My goal is to present you with four essential tips to writing truthful memoir and securing that blockbuster book deal, and that's why you're here, right?

You want tips?

I got tips.

Four of them:

TELLING THE TRUTH IN PERSONAL MEMOIR ★ TIP ONE

Remember: It Is True Because You Wrote It

I wrote the snippet below when I was twenty-two years old. I remember writing it. Thus, it is memoir. Be sure that you are sitting down when you read it:

> Occurrences are not alone and we are not apart from that which does occur if only when the stars are out and waters rise to lunar songs of times before they knew the moon was earth to men in solemn cubes of blueish light on evening rides with relatives and closer friends than even neighbors are
>
> Again
>
> The night it came when old men drank in musty bars and cherry bombed the bathrooms until laughter struck the night and whiskey breaths puffed home to lukewarm meals and upset women's hearts until morning drenched the sky and woke the men who panted off to work
>
> so that they can drive you home in emblemmed cars so neighbors can peek out and wonder where the lady had gone wrong.

Jesus Christ, what was I thinking?

In fact, I was high as a kite when I wrote those words. Stoned solid. I used a manual Royal typewriter because it made me feel more like Hemingway. Lived alone in a shotgun apartment back then. My best friend was the neighbor's scruffy cat, Ajax. Is *emblemmed* even a word?

HELPFUL WRITING PROMPT

Score some medical marijuana, regress to a fetus-like twenty-two-year-old, get an old typewriter on eBay, and connect with your pain.

Remember: Fiction Has Its Own Sort of Truth

So here's the odd thing. Underneath my weed-induced crimes against prose, reproduced above, there really was something that I was trying to get at. Something about my father's severe alcoholism—he was a stagger-home-every-night-drunk-at-midnight-from-the-corner-tavern sort of drunk—and about my mother's less obvious problems with drinking. One line omitted from my juvenilia above—". . . And times then came when women drove in drunken fear through whitened roads of shining hopes and banks of snowy fantasies until the metal touched and ripped and ran . . ."—refers to a real event, wherein my mom, way too soused to be behind the wheel, insisted on driving home anyway from a Christmas party with me in the backseat, only to sideswipe four cars on Eighth Street, during a near whiteout. The rest of that quasi-sentence—". . . and wandered to a formal place where pistoled men write funny words and listen to their radios . . ."—refers to what happened next. Instead of stopping, or turning right onto Cranberry and slowly driving the two blocks that would take us home, my mom drove another two miles to City Hall, where she promptly turned herself in at the main police station.

True.

Weird.

Couldn't have made it up.

Twenty-five years later—roughly thirteen years after writing my emblematic "Howl"—I had switched somehow from wanting to be Allen Ginsberg when I grew up to wanting to become Raymond Carver. (The growing-up part remained elusive.)

So, one day, I changed the model of automobile, the name of the town, the details of the sideswipe, and my first name and presented my child-hood memory in a short story titled "Just Tell Me What Happens Next":

It is December, a week shy of Christmas . . . A snow flurry has moved into the Cumberland Valley, light but steady, and the road is visible only about twenty feet from the Corvair's front headlights.

My mother drives down a narrow street, soft flakes rushing past the edges of our car, as if we are driving through a tunnel. Heat pours from the car's dashboard, and I lean forward in my seat, trying to see where we are headed.

My mother gazes into the snow, gripping the steering wheel with both hands. No one else seems to be on the road, although once, as we round the corner onto Fourth Street, I hear the clank of tire chains.

The streetlights shine yellow, making the snow seem less than real. My mother slows down some after the Corvair hits an icy patch and fishtails.

"You okay?" I ask her.

"Don't worry, Russ honey. Your mom can drive."

"Where are we going?"

"I don't know."

I see Chambersburg's main intersection a half-block ahead, and though the car is only creeping at this point, I brace myself against the dash. My mother applies the brakes a few feet before the stop sign, but the road is slick, uncertain. Her small, red hands wrestle the steering wheel as we slide to a stop, a few feet beyond the sign.

"You okay, honey?"

I don't answer.

"It's just a little icy, baby. Just a little icy."

"We should go home," I say.

"A little icy."

My mother inches the Corvair through the snow again, trying to make the turn. "I'm a little tipsy," she tells me.

"Why don't we walk?"

"Mommy's just tipsy. It doesn't mean she can't drive."

So far so good, yes? Forward movement, characterization, the child's limited point of view. Plus almost all of those are complete sentences, and I haven't made up a single word.

I count that as progress.

Here's a bit more:

I see it coming. My mother maneuvers the Corvair too close to a line of parked cars and bounces off the side fender of someone's station wagon. Again, the Corvair skids on the ice and comes to a stop in the middle of the road.

"Shit," she whispers. "My luck."

"Let's walk," I say again. "Leave the car here."

"I'm fine," my mother insists, but even at ten I can tell that she is straining to sound calm, in control. "Just have to go more slowly."

One last time, my mother moves the car along the whitened pavement, but the snow grows thicker, and I can barely see to the end of the hood. "I better park," she admits finally. "I think I hit someone's car."

I try by sheer mental will to direct the Corvair into one of the slanted parking spaces outside the Five and Dime. My mother manages to aim well enough into the slot, but isn't able to find the brake until the front half of the car is up over the curb and onto the sidewalk.

"Why?" she moans. "Why does it always have to snow?"

I see a red light flashing into the car and turn around in my seat; a black and white cruiser is directly behind us, and a man is already stepping out of the driver-side door. He comes around, aims his flashlight beam into the glass of my mother's window.

She rolls the window down. "Should have seen this coming," she mutters.

The officer stands slightly back, at attention, the flashlight beam held steady. In the dark, with the snow, and his light in our eyes, I can tell nothing about him except that he is tall.

"Marge," he says.

"Tom," my mother answers. It is a small town. We all know one another.

I remember meeting up once with George Plimpton, the great lion of New Journalism. I can't be sure what he said to me because I was stoned then as well. But maybe he said something like this:

"So, kid, if you really want to tell the truth, just write fiction. Memoir is for wieners. Do you want to be a wiener?"[1]

I didn't want to be a wiener, and that's why I wrote my story as fiction.

Do you want to be a wiener?

Does your wiener have a first name?

HELPFUL WRITING PROMPT

Write a truthful memory of your life. Then change key details to give the story more flow and rearrange the chronology of events to create a far more graceful and pleasing narrative arc. At the top of the first page, write: Fiction.

TELLING THE TRUTH IN PERSONAL MEMOIR ★ TIP THREE

Remember: You Can't Make This Shit Up

Many years later, Plimpton's prediction turned out to be false. I had become neither a wiener nor a fiction writer, it turned out, but one of America's Most Highly Respected Obscure Marginal Memoirists.

Believe me, I wear this badge with pride.

As a Respected but Obscure and Highly Marginal American Memoirist, it seemed there was a need for me to write about stuff that really

---

1. Some of these details may be misremembered.

happened—using my own name and honest-to-goodness details. What's that all about?

So anyway, I recycled the snowstorm story once again, but this time I told it straight, un-emblemmed and de-fictionalized.

Here is what came out:

My memory is of careening through a blizzard one Christmas Eve, my mother at the wheel. No one should have been out driving that night, given the visibility, but more to the point, my mother was drunk—so bombed that she eventually scraped the front bumper of our family Chevy across the side panels of two or three parked cars.

I was six or so. "Don't worry," my mother kept telling me. "I'm all right."

But she wasn't, and she knew it.

We were a block from our house when it finally dawned on Mom that skimming metal to metal against a line of parked cars was not acceptable, no matter how much snow was falling, or what the holiday. Her response was to drive two miles out of her way, straight down snow-drifted West 8th Street, to the City Hall police station. Once there, she turned herself in.

The officers behind the desk, perhaps already caught up in their own Christmas Eve revelry, seemed to find my mother's predicament amusing. I don't remember, but I'm guessing they took down the pertinent information. Or maybe they didn't. It was Christmas after all.

Thus we have come full circle.

And the lesson here, my writer friends?

If you want to write good, use empty transitional phrases like "thus we have come full circle," because even though these phrases may be meaningless, they sound awfully nice, and people often nod thoughtfully in response, because the words are soothing and familiar.

Consider this: If you *were* a wiener, if that is what you'd truly love to be, the whole world, with the likely exception of Muslims, kosher Jews, vegetarians, devout Hindus, and those on low-salt diets, would truly be in love with you. Now freewrite for thirty minutes from the point of view of an all-beef tube of meat. Take your freewriting and turn it into a memoir titled *Pray Love, Don't Eat Me!*

TELLING THE TRUTH IN PERSONAL MEMOIR * TIP FOUR

Remember: Two Moments and a Sense of Powerlessness

It is now roughly thirty-three years since I wrote the words "occurrences are not alone and we are not apart from that which does occur . . ." and I still don't understand them. It is roughly twenty-two years since I subsequently wrote the short story based on my mother's drunk-driving escapade. (And I still don't understand her.) It is roughly eight years since I took this memory and attempted to re-create it in memoir.

What do I really remember?

I have what I believe to be a reliable memory of a moment—almost a flash, a photographic instant—on Eighth Street, in my hometown, in a heavy snowstorm. I can see through my six-year-old eyes the cars parked along the north side of the road, and I remember my fear and confusion when my mother chose to drive on to the police station. I have a second flash of memory: the one where we are pulling in front of our house, on Ninth Street, in a police cruiser, and hoping against hope that none of the neighbors would be looking out their window and witnessing the latest Moore family embarrassment.

I have an emotional memory as well, of feeling powerless. I probably—though in truth, now I am out of the realm of verifiable memory and well into speculation, but speculation based on knowing very well what sort of a boy I was back then—said something like, "Mom, is that a good idea?" just quietly enough that she could ignore me if she wished.

Which she did, more or less. I feel pretty sure that she answered me—"Don't worry, I'm okay"—but she kept driving.

That's about it.

Those two moments and a sense of powerlessness. The rest I remember remembering years later, years ago, when I pieced it all together in my mind.

Memory is like a rope, knotted every three or four feet and hanging down a deep well. When you pull it up, just about anything might be attached to those knots. But you'll never know what's there if you don't pull. And the more you pull at that rope, the more you find.

Your memory rope may not contain a precise, photographic accounting of past events, because those moments become lost within seconds of anything that occurs. But still, your honest (if not accurate) memories will be attached to those knots, and those honest memories—along with reflection, examination, reconsideration—are precisely what the memoirist has to offer.

HELPFUL WRITING PROMPT

Enroll immediately in a summer writing workshop on some pastoral, semi-abandoned liberal arts campus, one with benches and trees. Study "The Art of Memoir" with a Respected but Obscure and Highly Marginal American Memoirist. Ask repeatedly, "What is creative about creative nonfiction? Doesn't 'creative' mean that I can change things?" Wait until the instructor collapses backward in his or her chair, defeated, ready to abandon all hope of ever explaining to you what is truthful about memoir, and then smile broadly and shout, "I was only kidding, silly goose!"

Meaningless Concluding Paragraphs

Remember that the time and energy you invest in your memoir doesn't end once you revise the final page, or even after the manuscript has been edited, produced, and published. There are lawsuits yet to come, plus lengthy interviews to be posted on blogs that no one ever reads.

And here are some final tips:

Supercharge your memoir with strong verbs and magnetically charged nouns. Use adverbs rarely and sparingly. If you are a movie star, be sure to mention that on page one. *Emblemmed* is not a word. Avoid familiar metaphors like the plague. Avoid the plague. Readers love sex, so consider traveling house to house with your book and a pack of condoms.

Remember, too, that the difference between an adequate word and the perfect word is like the difference between a lightning bug and a runaway fuel tanker exploding on I-95. The role of a writer is not to say what we all can say but to say what we all can say in such a way that the writer garners the interest of a high-powered literary agent.

When writing long passages of exposition, consider using abbreviations.

And finally, remember that if *you* don't tell your story, no one will. Which might be just fine.

Dinty W. Moore

On "Four Essential Tips for Telling the Truth . . ."

Implementing Exaggeration and Humor

I have always been intrigued by humorists but find myself torn as to where they fall in the spectrum of genre. Humor writers like Dorothy Parker, Robert Benchley, James Thurber, and David Sedaris allow themselves certain over-the-top exaggerations for comic effect, and thank goodness for that. But at what point does exaggeration become, well, no longer nonfiction?

I do think that discerning readers can usually detect when a memory is being pushed to an outer limit for humorous effect, though not always.

My goal with this piece (a goal I didn't discover until the sixteenth draft, by the way, since I always stumble into a new writing project half-blind and fully disoriented) was to play with that borderland—exaggeration and humor—yet also say something true about the various nonfiction genre controversies. What is "creative" about creative nonfiction?

What does "truth" mean in memoir? Do "fake" memoirs, like James Frey's stupid book *A Million Little Pieces*, tar the whole genre?

Essayists Brenda Miller and Suzanne Paola once wrote about what they call "hermit crab essays," pieces of writing that—like the actual crustacean bearing the name—move from one shell to the shell of another. Their examples included essays written in the form of crossword puzzles, horoscopes, or letters to the editor. Beth Ann Fennelly, in her essay earlier in this book, reflects on her own experiments with the "hermit crab essay." I decided to let my "hermit crab" move into the shell of a "How to Write Your Book in Four Easy Steps" article sometimes found in writing magazines. That made more room for funny, I think.

And by the way, the memory of my mother driving in the snowstorm is entirely true, and the pieces of my early writing I share are word-for-word true as well. What I mean is, they are what I wrote back then, though obviously the short story version has many details changed. I did meet George Plimpton, numerous times, but he probably didn't say that thing about being a wiener. I'm likely kidding about that.

And I do think the author has an obligation to pull on that knotted rope of memory and report accurately on what comes up from the well. Is memory flawed? Yes, but if what you are writing purports to be nonfiction, you need to present an honest account of your memory, flaws and all.

Now, get to work.

Susan Neville

A Visit to the Doctor

When the man in Room Seven goes to see his doctor, he always wears a baseball cap and jacket.

He's in here to get the results of the MRI.

The X-ray shows compression in the spine, a slight fracture.

That might radiate to the left hip, his doctor said, his mind already moving down the hall to his next patient. Does the pain seem to radiate?

No, the man answers.

The shorter the sentences, the more likely the doctor will hear him.

His wife reads from her notebook. Methodist South. Third floor. MRI.

The man in Room Seven was a tail gunner in World War II. Pow! Pow! MRI.

Strafe doctor with short sentences. Make him pay attention.

The doctor held on to the computer keyboard to keep from bolting down the hallway, toward another room and another, toward his office, toward the papers in the office, demanding signatures, phone lights blinking, beeper buzzing, consultations, the wife and children, perhaps a mistress to calm him down.

They're on the same hunk of rock but time is moving at different speeds.

Eighty-five years ago I jumped out an eighty-sixth-floor window, and the ground is about ten inches from my face now. I need an answer, stat.

But the doctor is already out the door, down the hallway. Nurses hand him papers as he flies by.

Necrotic hip, he says. Ball in the socket. Like walking on a fracture. Should I walk?

Don't. How can you walk on a necrotic hip?

But he's been in rehab for weeks being told to walk, his wife explains. We just got him home! For four weeks they told him to practice walking. He did. The physical therapist comes to the house now and tells him to walk. Lazy bum, they all said. Walk, you lazy bum.

He can't, the doctor said.

He has to, his wife said. She is too small to lift him otherwise.

If he doesn't walk, he'll get weak, she says. If he gets weak, he won't move. If he doesn't move, he'll get pneumonia again. If he gets pneumonia, he'll go to the hospital. If he goes to the hospital, he'll get weaker. If he gets weaker, they'll send him to Room Seven again. If they send him to Room Seven, they'll tell him to walk in order to get home.

The doctor isn't listening. What can the doctor do? He sees this patient and the next and the next and then he goes home and the next day it begins all over.

Every day is catastrophe.

There were German subs on duty in the Atlantic. We sailed on a Liberty Ship to Naples, Italy. We took an English boat to Taranto in southern Italy and were based in San Pancrazio. We had little heat in the barracks, just an oil drum that fed oil through copper tubing into the barracks where it dripped into a fifty-five-gallon drum set on bricks. We had a small coffee can set in the bottom next to a side opening in the drum. The oil flow was adjusted so it would drip enough to burn constantly without overflowing.

The food at the mess was very good. Fresh-baked bread for every meal and SPAM prepared in different ways. On the ship I had learned to hate mutton and tea containing cream.

We took out railroad marshaling yards in Austria, blew up bridges in the Brenner Pass. We flew between mountains to hit bridges. Enemy flak guns would hit at eye level. *Fighter planes were thick before and after we hit Vienna. We lost several planes and returned to base with two hundred to three hundred holes in the plane.*

We were asked if we wanted a two-ounce bottle of bourbon when we returned in the afternoon or if we wanted a whole fifth when we completed our thirty-five missions. We elected for the fifth.

And here I am now, moving between home and the doctor's offices and Room Seven with my wife as escort. When I am in Room Seven, my wife smuggles in airplane bottles of Dewar's. She thinks I don't know that she's watered them down. I know the taste of bourbon.

But the doctor is already standing. The wife keeps a list of her husband's medicines in her purse. The two of them hold on to each other's birth dates like a rope. 8/12/25 and 7/06/30. Forget those numbers and you're dead. Carve the date you forget them on a stone. Mr. Schaefer? Mrs. Schaefer? Do you know your birthdates? Do you know where you are?

This doctor, the one running in and out the door, is in the middle of his life. He's gathered too many patients and he knows it. He is temporarily the crown of his creation. All around him, sparrows fall. Look at me! Soon his family will fall apart because of the hours he spends at work. Look at me! He will find a new wife and family. He does not know that yet.

When the doctor leaves the room, the man moves his wheelchair toward the door and puts his coat over his shoulders. Open the door, he tells his wife.

He sits in the open door in the line of patient examining rooms, looking out in the hallway for the doctor. If all the patients stood in their doorways looking out, they could see each other. They could look out like a line of whores in a red-light district. They could clock the doctor's speed. They would see how he runs. They could feel the pressure of time roaring in the painted corridor.

You in a hurry? the doctor jokes when he comes back to the open door with the prescription.

The old man sits in the wheelchair and wears his World War II vet baseball cap.

I don't have much time, the old man says, but the doctor doesn't hear it.

What was the word he used? his wife asks on the way out. I want to write it down.

Necrotic, he tells her.

She still has her purse in her hand, and she takes out her notebook and pen.

Yesterday, when the sleet fell and froze and then the ten inches of snow fell on top of it, she had walked out to the mailbox. Eighty-years old, and she let the garage door up and held on to the side of the house, pulling herself around to the icy, snow-covered yard. She dug in one heel and then the other, walked on her heels all the way out for the paper.

How do you spell the word? she asks.

He watches as she writes.

Having written the word down meant she could ask her son-in-law the doctor what it meant and how to fix it. She still has faith that he could do that.

You don't need to ask him, the man from Room Seven says. Necropolis, necrophilia, necrosis. It all means death.

He tells me I'll never walk, he continues.

That's not what he said.

It's what he was saying. I got the answer to today's question. Today's question was the hip. The hip is dead.

Don't drive that way, he says, when she turns left. The other way.

There are an infinite number of ways to get home. There isn't a correct way.

She drops the prescription off at the drive-through. Percocet. Next it will be Vicodin, then morphine.

We'll order one of those swiveling chairs, she says, those hovering chairs. Medicare pays for them. All of it. The chair that lifts. The bed that raises and lowers.

Not in my damn house, he says. None of that looking like a hospital. What is the pain in his hip? Arterial necrosis.

He was hoping the answer would be arthritis. He was hoping for a shot of steroids.

Instead, he'd been pushed to walk for weeks because no one had told him that there was nothing there to walk with. No ball in the hip joint.

He is a disintegrating skeleton with too much flesh to carry.

When the body flew, it flew in leather jackets lined with wool.

In Brenner Pass they flew between mountains to hit bridges and enemy flak guns hit them at eye level. They were in the air! They could have rammed into the mountains. But his pilot was skilled. His pilot was twenty-one. His pilot was the oldest in the crew. The skies were beautiful. Anvil-shaped clouds. They were a flying coffin filled with beautiful boys.

On the next mission, we were hit hard as we entered the final bombing phase of the run. Sure enough, this gunner bailed out through the open bomb bay doors.

At the instant he bailed, about half the bombers dropped their bombs. We were in advance of the actual release point.

The bombs hit the Vienna Opera House. Ninety-five percent of the building was destroyed, and all the props. Two hundred fifty thousand props, including scenery and costumes, including music stands and instruments. This is the one mission we didn't talk about.

The building was filled with frescoes one hundred years old. The costumes and props on fire. It had been built carefully, with the finest stone.

He was the top musician in his high school. He has a medal from his high school band director. He has the Air Medal with three oak-leaf clusters. He has the ETO ribbon with five battle stars. He has a Purple Heart. He has a medal of gratitude from Yugoslavia. He had a ball in the hip joint then.

When the ice has melted enough that the streets are clear, his children drive down to his house. His son the doctor, his son the doctor's girlfriend, his daughter the teacher, and her husband the psychologist.

You father's asleep, the wife says to his children. He's been asleep all day. It's the Percocet.

The man from Room Seven is slumped in his chair while the others eat cubed steak and frozen corn and homemade mashed potatoes. There is a German chocolate cake and a cranberry salad. There are fresh rolls and butter and sweet tea and a bottle of local wine. There is an illusion of normalcy, of festivity, a bowl of beer nuts and a plate of cheese and crackers.

Did he see his children enter? Did he smell the food?

He doesn't look right, his wife says. The man in the chair makes a sound. His wife goes over to him as if talking to a child.

Do you need to go to the bathroom? she asks. He is heavy, but where is the heaviness? His bones are deteriorating, but he is still a sack of rocks balanced on what used to be a hip. He can't feel his knee. He breathes out the word knee. He balances on the walker and the two men and they get him moving.

Outside the window, the yard was filled with catalpa beans that had fallen on top of the ice and snow. The beans are leathery and curved and there are small sticks in the yard. It looks like driftwood, like a beach where an ancient weathered boat has disintegrated and washed ashore. The wife can't wait until the snow has melted and the warm weather comes. She wanted to pick up the seeds and sticks and have them carted away.

The man begins getting the walker wheels to move. The knee holds, and a kind of momentum takes hold as well as they move toward the bedroom. The oxygen tube curls across the floor and the daughter moves it like a bridal train. They are all his attendants now. He makes it to the bathroom, and the wife shoos them away. She gets him inside, pants around his knees, helps him lower himself and leaves to give him privacy. When she returns he is unresponsive. Still breathing. Still sitting up.

He doesn't know her. Then he knows her. Then he doesn't know her.

She returns to the living room. Go help your father, she says to his son, the doctor. The son disappears with him and comes out in a short while with his father on the walker seat. The son is smiling. All is well. This is the way it goes.

Take him to the dining room, his wife says.

The sun is setting on snow. The room is gray in the evening. Ice in the glasses, ice on the sidewalks, inches of snow and frozen sleet on the grass.

Normal conversation, glances at the old man. Usually he would have saved stories for this occasion, would have long, complicated jokes to tell, jokes that were so verbally complex, with so many twists and turns that you had to pay attention or you'd miss the punch line.

Swallow, the son's girlfriend reminds the man when it seems he has forgotten. She keeps a close eye on him. It's important, the others decide, that we continue to talk. This is what human beings do around a table.

I'm going to cut the pills in half, the wife says. She's looking at her husband with his mouth full of food and it going nowhere. Now and then in the past few months there have been flashes of the man she married on his face. He'll start to get angry and then stick his tongue out at her like a boy. She'll stick her tongue right back at him. Nyah

nyah. Do kids still do that? At the edge of all of this, this life, when they want to kill each other or run away, they laugh and turn back into it. Nyah nyah. Now there's a dab of something on his chin. John, she says. He hears his name. His name!

John, the old man hears. Dad. He spits whatever's in his mouth into the girlfriend's napkin.

The actual daughter couldn't do that, couldn't help him to the bathroom or pick him up from the floor or hold her napkin under his chin. What can she do? Health really is another country, where sickness can't be imagined. Sickness requires a different landscape than this noise and gaiety. When she's sick she wants clean sheets. White sheets. Colors make her worse. Darkness and silence if the illness is in the stomach, or if it's pain. Sunlight if it's the flu or a cold. No television. No strangers talking. Sometimes, rare times, the bed feels like it's floating in light and returning to health, the first day out of bed, she wants to go back to it.

They sing happy birthday to the girlfriend. They eat German chocolate cake.

Isn't this fun, Dad?

The father is still asleep.

The world is an aquarium, and he has become the fish, or the little plastic man with scuba gear in the pebbles at the bottom of the tank. His teeth are in pink tubs on the hospital's bedside tray. His mouth is sunken in, the jaw hanging open to the right so he looks, perpetually, like the man in *The Scream*. He's in an aquarium, his skin like scales. In every room there are other large beached fish. He sees them when he is wheeled in. In some of the rooms are fish with their mouths open in Os. Someone has removed the hooks. So much work the teeth do to determine the structure of the face. Such a handsome man he was. Is this what happens to one at eighty?

All the rooms are single now. It's better this way. The messiness of a roommate, the person next to you a stranger but dripping bodily fluids across the floor, bacteria and viruses increasing exponentially, the odd sounds in the nighttime, the wife who sleeps in a chair and washes out her linens in the sink, the family squabbles. The respect for humans here. The respect that's due him. There's a foldout couch and, by the window, a small desk for visitors' laptops. It's like a nice hotel room.

Still.

The nurses are kind. Will he see a doctor? It doesn't matter.

Perhaps they will forget he's here, simply take care of him in this solicitous way for days, for weeks, months, however long it takes until he's young again.

He can't think about the future. He will go home where life will be hard and he will be hard on his wife and the children will take turns spending the night.

He thinks about his sister and his father and his mother. He thinks about his pilot and navigator. When his mother was in the hospital during her last illness the floors were linoleum. The walls were white. She would smile at him when he came in.

I was just thinking, she'd say, how everything in here originally came from something natural. They sat there tracing each thing back to its source, as mineral or plant. Linoleum? What is that? How proud he was to have a mother like that. In the summer she would lie on the grass and watch the cottonwood seeds emerge from the blue. She would watch for hours. Fireworks, sparks, oh gorgeous universe.

What would she think of him now, her blue-eyed boy?

Susan Neville

On "A Visit to the Doctor"

The Omission of I

I'm not quite sure myself where the boundaries are between fiction and nonfiction, but I'm sure the boundaries need to be tested. The meaning you try to make out of a thing is always a combination of tradition and innovation; we can't stay where we were without risking stupidity and we can't move forward without risking stupidity. So risk stupidity. I'm sure there are more innovative borders that involve forms beyond these two, but the question I still have about the essay is where the I is located, whether it can be implied, and how close the observer/essayist can get, through empathy or the imagination, to the interiority of another.

And so this is an essay about my father. Sections in italics were written by him. I was in the doctor's office and at the party. I interviewed both the doctor and my brother about how a medical practice lives and dies. I would say that all of this is based on what was said or what I observed. The easiest way to write this piece would have been to include that I. But I removed my subjective self from the exploration and focused on other subjectivities. I relied, at times, on observation of a gesture to reveal the interior, and I gave myself the freedom to imagine the thoughts they revealed. I'm not sure, still, whether an essayist should do that. Calling this fiction would remove that problem. But my intention was not to write fiction. It was to write a historically accurate portrait and to explore an idea about the relationship between doctor and patient and mortality. Both of those intentions lie in the realm of nonfiction.

What is gained and what is lost by removing the I? I'm not sure that, in the final product, it matters. It's all in the process, in the way you can get closer to what feels true. It's all shadow boxing. Still, there's that annoying tone of narcissism that is part of memoir writing I suppose. It felt good to get outside of that. None of these scenes were about me, finally, and getting beyond the *me*, seeing others in the fullness of their selves, is essential. An insistence on the I made its way into the social sciences as well as literary prose in the twentieth century as a means of arguing that there is no such thing as an objective truth. That point has been made now. On the other hand, there has to be something between traditional journalism and self-absorption. I'm interested in exploring what that something is.

Brian Oliu

Contra

In your first life, you were foolish—running where you shouldn't be running, crashing into trees, touching everything you saw. In your next life, you were more cautious—ducking when things were thrown your way, jumping over crevasses. In your next life, the sky started to fall in—talons of birds you have never seen in any of your lives. In the lives after that you began to understand the world that you were placed in: that things, terrible things, can come at you from behind, from underneath. To be swept off one's feet only to fall again from the sky, curled up in a ball, rotating. When I saw you, surrounded, you were aware of the names of things—you knew that when you jumped you could move back and forth in midair like a balloon, like wings, like spiraling. You knew what things to touch—wings that fell from the sky like you once did after the sixteenth time that you died, wings that would make you stronger—wings that allowed you to remove self from self, to streak ahead of your body like a flashlight, turning all things to white. In this life, you do not know the world that we live in. You do not know how quickly the seasons change, how fast it can go from leaves as thick as bulbs, from snakes moving with a quickness, from mosquitoes biting your white legs while we sit in the backyard. You look like the type that smokes cigarettes: you will not let me light it for you. In a past life, you would have let me come closer, would have let me bring my hand as close to your mouth as possible without touching it, allowing you to breathe on my hand before snapping your neck upward and exhaling. You are always looking up. You are always pressing your chin to your chest while you walk, as if you can see through the ground that we walk on, as if there is something in the water. There is always something in the water: there is nothing I can do about this. Believe me when I say that I am the only one: I do not control the fire. I do not control the mouths on doors, the sickles. Yet you blame me for it. You blame me for being here: for the roaches that try to crawl into your ears while you sleep, that cause you to forget how to exhale, how to breathe on my hand. You heard a story about their white blood, about living on without a head, about how they will run to your hands if you have been cutting onions for soup. Do not worry about these things. Do not worry about your eyelashes being eaten while you are sleeping. Do not worry about the rat that lived underneath my crib when I was a child, about how it would scale the bedpost like you climbing up to where the water falls. These are things to worry about elsewhere. These are for future lives to worry about. You, in your new life have no time to rest. Rest is a number. To talk is a number. This has nothing to do with change, with having to get to work, with throwing an onion at your back. I do not know if you have time to sit down: to have a meal, to talk about things — the world you are trying to save, the people you are trying to defend. I am scared to touch your hand in fear that you might die. I am scared to make a noise in fear that I might die. When you leave here, you will step incorrectly. You will fall from the sky like you always do. You will start running forward. You will restart where you fell, circling — the yard, the kitchen. You will keep going and you will remember none of this — how you got out of this building, why you arrived, why all of the roaches are dead, why it is snowing, why we are wearing white. If you were to remember me, you would remember me as faceless. You would remember my motions — where I arrived from, when I jumped, what patterns I made. You would remember that you cannot touch me, or else you would fall to the ground. I would tell you that to touch my skin is worth dying a twenty-third time, a twenty-fourth, a twenty-fifth. This is what I was running toward you to tell you. This is why you laid me to waste.

Brian Oliu

On "*Contra*"

Nostalgia and the Shared Experience

I've never been one for categorization—I consider myself primarily a nonfiction writer, but others might see me as a poet or that some of my work that relies heavily on extended metaphor is fictional. I can't write characters or plot, I write exclusively from my own experiences, and I don't understand line breaks, so I always use the term *lyric essay* or *piece*. To me, the difference between prose poetry and flash fiction is in the eye of the writer: what the writer set out to write is what it is in the end. Of course the reader will attach his or her own ideas. I think of Carolyn Forche's "The Colonel," which I've taught in a lyric essay course, a prose course, and a poetry course, and there are wonderful things to say about it from multiple angles.

"Contra" is from a series of lyric essays based off of eight-bit Nintendo games—I view these pieces as "game collaborations": ways of telling personal stories through a work of fiction, although there is something interactive and universal about games. In a way, video games are a new version of fairy tales: we remember exactly where we were when we defeated Ganon with the silver arrows, when we captured fairies in jars. There is an element of nostalgia that comes with playing games, and while thinking about them, all sorts of memories come back: where you played the game for the first time, the feeling you got when you beat a game. We are not actually Little Red Riding Hood, we remember fear when walking alone, we remember our grandmothers' houses. Similarly, we are not Bill or Lance blasting our way through an alien heart, but we remember the frustration of dying over and over again; the time we heard that there was a code to give the player thirty lives, a way to trick the system and finally see the game to its end. There is an ownership in video games: we use the phrase "I have only one life left" instead of "my character has only one life left," and as a result we have a shared experience, sometimes even a connection to this fictional character made up of pixels, who jumps and spins and is vulnerable, always vulnerable.

Lia Purpura

Squirrel

An *Ars Poetica*

Today, in her front yard, my neighbor found a baby squirrel that had fallen out of its nest. Her five-year-old daughter showed it to me, sleeping in a cigar box, and said they were taking it to a wildlife rescue center out in the country. They were going to make a day of it, and go for lunch and take a nice walk. I remembered, then, the nest of baby mice we found when I was pregnant and how we brought them to Gerta, a wildlife nurse, who pledged not to feed them to the owls she also rescued. And how she rigged up a little incubator with a bare lightbulb over a cotton-filled bowl for the pink, squirming things.

Now, today, seven years after those mice, seeing the baby squirrel, I thought: how excessive. That the world, certainly the neighborhood, doesn't need another squirrel, that we recently paid to have five of them trapped and evicted from our attic. How only for her daughter is she doing this. A good lesson. Kind instruction in the care of small, hurt things. I imagined finding the squirrel, walking by it in the tall grass under the pine tree in the yard—and leaving it there. Just letting it go. Passing it by. Passing it over.

I don't think I'll be the old woman who walks with her hands clasped behind her back through fall leaves—bent, contemplative, at peace. Though I might be, because, really, I don't know what an old woman thinks. What she's done. Who she's been.

Soon after my talk with my neighbor, my son called from a friend's house to say they'd found a baby squirrel and could he keep it. And please, Mom, please.

Long pause on my end.

Mom?

I'm thinking, I said.

And then I went to get it. I brought a shoebox.

And yes, of course I did this for my son. It's that time of year, the wildlife rescue guy told my neighbor. The time of year for what? For runs to the store for eyedroppers, for chopping sunflower seeds, for fashioning shredded napkin nests? For first deaths? I nudged its mouth open and gave it some water squeezed from a washcloth. Then I left the squirrel on the porch in the box.

And what kind of mother am I, taking the thing in knowing what I know. Letting it go by such mild neglect, blaming it on the cat in whose mouth, soft mouth, they found the squirrel.

"This wasn't the way I planned to spend the afternoon," said my neighbor.

This *was* the way I planned to spend the afternoon, I thought: writing.

Lia Purpura

On "Squirrel: An Ars Poetica"

Starting in One Place and Ending in Another

I do not mean to be noncompliant and mess up the project here, but I am not of a mind to comment on my own work. Why don't I want to comment? (In *general* I mean—it's not *you*, dear editors, readers, and friends!) Because what looks in the *end* like a coherent piece, *wasn't* for a long time, so to suggest that my decisions, or problems and solutions, form a trail that in some way might be followed by another feels disingenuous. Not true to the micro-movements I made in un-selfconscious ways.[1] Those moves weren't drawn from a pot of solutions, but rather, such decisions along the way were impromptu and related to very specific moments of making. Moments do not harbor "problems"—it doesn't feel that way at all to me. I can't seem to turn myself into a hindsight assessor. I don't track the fits and starts or keep a log of rough spots for future discussion. Or for pedagogical purposes.

---

1. Other thoughts on my resistance: (a) I have a lousy memory and can't recall what happened where and to play strictly by the rules set forth here, I'd have to patch together something about the "process" I went through and that feels like cheating. (b) I fear that going through drafts and tracing the lifecycle of, say, a paragraph would be colossally boring/fussy/solipsistic. It is important, however, to know that a paragraph (a line, a specific word, punctuation even) *has* a life cycle and that by writing one becomes intimate with the options available (cut, cut back, build up, move around, splice in, hold in reserve, etc.). Those early drafts of Elizabeth Bishop's "One Art," for instance, teach me *nothing* about *how* she moved the poem along from an early prosey sketch into the gorgeous thing is it now—but it does assure me, in the most basic and primitive way, that at one time the gorgeous thing *was* a wild and messy sketch. That greatness grows from humble beginnings—I'm never tired of learning that. That sustains me.

I bump into something, try a lot of different things, it dissolves into rightness or near-rightness or stays wrong.

I don't mean to be ornery.

After one essay's finished, should I have more to say on the subject, I'll start another essay and pick up the thread, meander forth, try another tack. Maybe that's helpful . . . to say: after you finish one essay, go write another one. And make your *own* decisions and work through your *own* difficulties by way of *practice*, because that's what it is to write. Be alert to unfinished business. Sure, sometimes there are interesting backstories to essays (exactly how I came to do research on autopsies, for instance, is usually of interest to readers of *On Looking*), but that's just party talk.

This essay is an *ars poetica*: a statement about the art as I practice it.

It "bends genres" (I'm trying hard to answer the question I was assigned now, thus the quoted phrase) because an *ars poetica* is supposed to be a *directive* or *manifesto-like*, *sure-footed*, even *screedish*—and this just kind of *wanders into* the form. Slips in sideways. Backdoors it. Behaves like a very brief essay. It's even sort of koan-like. I did not set out to write it as such; I was just sketching out a singular moment. I like ending up with something I had no intention of doing. Trying for something I have grave doubts about. Having no idea what it is I'm after, for a very long time. Assuming that anything I sit down to is "just a sketch." That's tremendously freeing.

Wendy Rawlings

Why I Hope My Soap Opera
Will Outlive Me and Other
Confessions about a Dying Art

This is a genre, unlike all others, that requires
one thing of its audience—its memory, its collective recollection of who you are and what
you've done. That is extraordinary.

Charles Keating, "Carl Hutchins," *Another World*

They are very separate entities but attributes of
each affecting the other. I don't believe that you
can play a character for 31 years and not have
parts of the character affect you and vise versa.

"CM," via e-mail with me

According to *The Guinness Book of World Records*, *General Hospital* is the
longest-running soap opera currently in production, having aired more
than twelve thousand episodes. Let's just write that out numerically:
12,000 (!!!). On soap operas, as opposed to, say, sitcoms, characters acquire long and deep and complex histories not unlike the long and deep
and complex histories humans acquire after living for a few decades.
Soap viewers watch these histories accrue in what seems to be real time.

When I first started watching GH in 1979, the technology to connect me with other viewers didn't exist. The technology to record an
episode and watch it later that day didn't even exist. In the thirty years
since I started watching, VCRs, DVRs, Facebook, Twitter, chat rooms,

fan pages, YouTube, and dozens of other innovations have allowed fans like me to sink more deeply into our soaps than we would have been able to imagine.

> Sad, sad show =(hope you guys aren't crying to hard
> (lldubs [Laura Wright, "Carly," G H], via Twitter)

> Join my drama free gh group where its totally drama free and u dont have to worry bout being bashed or attacked for stating ur opinion or liking characters someone else dis like....
> (RachaelmzRayonce' Davis,[1] via Facebook)

> how selfish was carho[2] today she at least cud of game jason[3] a couple days before asking him for jake[4] kidney i mean dame women the man son just died probley an hour before she asked him that and joss[5] aint goin no where anytime soon so she cud of gave it time before asking him and wtf she asking jason for anyway jason is not his legal father so he cant just give jake kidney away if he wanted to thats up to liz[6] and lucky[7]....today was an emotional day by the way

---

1. I "met" Rachael, a very opinionated black nineteen-year-old in Chicago, via a *General Hospital* fan page she started on Facebook called "The RachaelmzRayonce' Davis Show." I have never met her face-to-face, but we comment on each other's posts daily.
2. Rachael's nickname for a character on *GH* named "Carly Jax." Carho = Carly + "ho" (whore). At least three times per day, usually apropos of nothing, Rachael posts on Facebook: "Dear *GH*: Kill Carho!!!"
3. "Jason Morgan," hunky mob operative and important character on *GH*.
4. "Jake Webber," Jason's son, the product of an extramarital affair between Jason and Elizabeth Webber. Jason gave up his son in order to protect him from the dangers of the mob. On this week's episode, Jake is hit by a car and killed; thus, his kidney is up for grabs.
5. "Josslyn Jax," infant daughter of Carly Jax. She has just been diagnosed with a Wilms tumor and needs that kidney.
6. Elizabeth Webber, mother of Jake.
7. Lucky Spencer, former (cuckolded) husband of Elizabeth, who adopted Jake as his own.

love L&L2[8] scenes today

(RachaelmzRayonce' Davis, via Facebook)

Rachael has created Facebook pages devoted to *GH* such as "LANTE FOREVA" and "We want guza[9] fired!!!" Rachael's stated reason for starting the KILL CARLY page is "for all u cujo[10] haters please add ur friends to dis group so we can all express our hate for carly." I'm a member of this group, but I'm not a Carly hater. I sometimes feel a little creepy about the extent of Rachael's vitriol. I've wondered whether I should mention to her that I follow the actress who plays Carly, Laura Wright, on Twitter, and that I was delighted to discover that the actress owns Standing Sun Wines in California's Santa Ynez Valley, is a devoted wine drinker like I am, and recently lost fourteen pounds on Weight Watchers (I recently lost ten on same).

DEAR GH:

i think i need to take a break from dis show cuz I see its making me lose my religious I have neva said the HATE word or HATED anyone in my life until i start watching dis soap and i know its just a show and its not really real but i am starting to feel my hate towards cujo to the point I am wishing death upon her even tho shes just a character . . .[11]

Now, in addition to remembering thirty years of *GH* plot points, I'm in contact with other fans that possess the same *GH* memory bank

---

8. Even a die-hard *GH* fan like me can't understand all of Rachael's codes right away; like a good rapper, she's always reinventing the language. This probably refers to scenes between Lulu Spencer and Dante Falconeri, Rachael's raison d'etre for watching *GH*. Like many viewers, Rachael refers to popular couples by combining their first names. Thus, Dante and Lulu become "Lante."

9. Robert Guza Jr., head writer for *GH* on and off since 1996.

10. Another of Rachael's nicknames for Carly, this one taken from the title of Stephen King's novel about a rabid, murderous dog.

11. RachaelmzRayonce' Davis, via Facebook.

as I do. We follow the most popular GH actors on Twitter, where they tweet each other and certain lucky fans daily. Laura Wright, the much-maligned Carly, for instance, has 23,649 followers. Tweets among the actors segue seamlessly between their real lives and the lives of their characters. If you're a regular GH viewer, you have no trouble differentiating between the two and can feel pleasantly in on the joke when Nancy Lee Grahn, who plays Alexis Davis, tweets about the cleavage-revealing blue dress she wore to the big wedding.[12] In her next tweet, the actress might express her support for a Jewish feminist cause.[13]

On Twitter, GH actors have adopted the phrase "heading out to PC" or "going to Port Chuck"[14] when they tweet they're leaving home to work on the set of GH. Rarely do people say they're heading to set. Though Port Charles is an entirely fictional city, without a mayor or longitude or zip code, I do not intend to be coy in suggesting that Port Charles is a place we can go, a place so many of us have envisioned that in some sense it does exist. One of my favorite fan groups on Facebook is "Jake's Bar, Port Charles, New York & Port Charles, New Zealand." Named for a bar on the show where most of the characters drink, this group consists of viewers who post weary comments about the show's plot twists, as if we've all met up at a neighborhood bar to discuss that day's episode. One quirk of this page is that most people begin posting by narrating that they are pulling up a stool and then asking the bartender for a drink.[15] Sometimes of an evening I'll be so charmed

12. Sonny Corinthos and Brenda Barrett's long-awaited wedding on GH, of course.
13. Which I find a rather jarring moment of reality, since GH rarely gestures at ethnic, religious, or political identity, and since no one on GH, not even a mob lawyer named Bernie Abrahms, is overtly Jewish.
14. Port Charles, the fictional upstate New York city where GH is set. Another nickname: "The Chuckles," used primarily and ironically by an Australian character up from Down Under, Ethan Lovett, who finds the city provincial.
15. For instance, one fan notes: "BARTENDER I NEED A BOTTLE OF EVERY KINDA LIQUOR U HAVE WITH A COUPLE OF SHOT GLASSES. Its been one of those days 2day and 4 the past month."

by a conversation developing in real time over a series of posts that I'll go pour myself a glass of chardonnay.

95% of the ppl here cannot separate fiction from reality which is really sad and speaks of incompetence.
(A Fan, via Facebook)

There are moments when the depth of my immersion in this massive trove of GH minutiae and in this community that comprises one of the most pleasurable sources of leisure and diversion in my life is such that I forget all my own and other people's objections to being obsessed with a soap opera. Soaps are low culture, and fans' devotion to them is voyeuristic and parasitic: you're watching someone else's life rather than living your own. And yet, the nature of the serial is to give the impression of lives being lived slowly and minutely over many years, the way real lives are lived. Sometimes, while jogging, I'll be thinking about the show, and I'll wonder how far the Quartermaine mansion is from the docks where Kelly's Grill is located, or from the hospital, or from Baker Street (where violent crimes go down), or from Robin and Patrick's house. I'll be putting it together in my mind, filling in the park where Robin likes to take her baby Emma for a picnic, and the upscale Metrocourt Hotel that Carly and Jasper Jax own, and I'll have a realization I can only describe as shattering.

None of this exists.

I hesitate to say that the feeling is existential, but it reminds me of a feeling that would come over me at eleven or twelve, when I first fully came to understand that I was a being with a terminal life span, that I would one day die and be no more. There's a way in which *General Hospital* fills, for lack of a better term, the yawning chasm of nothingness that is my understanding of my own finitude.

Or at least it makes me less lonely.

There is a great need in human beings for other people's stories. You can follow a story for six weeks on a soap and learn a little something about different kinds of relationships, about life.

(Harding Lemay, former head writer, *Another World*)

I've been lonely since I was a girl, when my best friend and favorite cousin died of leukemia within three years of each other.[16] Born two-thirds of the way through the twentieth century, I've found the first part of the twenty-first century an even lonelier time than my adolescence was. My job as a college professor took me away from family and friends in New York to Tuscaloosa, Alabama. Perhaps it's my constitution as an introvert and a writer that makes me especially receptive to online communication as well as to the kind of voyeurism soap operas offer. The experience of watching GH, of following Nancy Lee Grahn on Twitter, and of posting comments on Facebook with other GH fans is all virtual: *that which is not real, but may display salient qualities of the real*. But I'm not sure anymore about how much the binary between real and virtual obtains. Though many people accuse Facebook of evacuating meaning from the word *friend*, I find that online communication has given me both a broader and more nuanced understanding of what friendship might mean. Some Facebook friends, people I've never met in real life, comment on my posts daily. We trade reading or movie suggestions, cheer each other on before running marathons or interviewing for jobs, and, well, engage in conversation about whether Josslyn Jax deserved to get Jake Spencer's kidney.

And some posters go further, inventing new narratives for GH characters:

16. This kind of coincidence, I discovered, is the meat-and-potatoes of soap operas, a fact I found strangely comforting, since people in my real life said they found the coincidence of two leukemia deaths "unbelievable."

Shoutout to CARHO i just went pass her house and saw THE MUF-
FIN MAN sneaking out the back door SMDH[17] if only he new wat
he just caught from that infested foam at the mouth BEAST!!![18]

This moment of Rachael inserting herself into the world of GH — being in the right place at the right time to witness a gentleman caller in-
fected with rabies from "Carho/Cujo," leaving via the back door (always
a sign of impropriety) — is pure invention yet satisfies Rachael's desire
to implicate Carly as a rabid whore and to be the canny tale teller who
knows and relays all of Port Charles's secrets. How our lives have bled
into our fictions; how our fictions come to create our lives. I posted a
question to Rachael: "Who is THE MUFFIN MAN?" She wrote back
almost immediately, "WHO LIVE ON JURY LANE?!" I had to go think
about this for a while before I figured out Rachael was referring to a
nursery rhyme:

Do you know the muffin man
the muffin man the muffin man.
Do you know the muffin man,
That lives in Drury Lane?

When I was young, my mother and I used to sing about the muffin
man who lived on Emerson Lane, since that was a nearby street where
my friend Denise Minicozzi lived. I never knew that the original street
was Drury Lane, which Rachael modified as "Jury." When I made this
discovery, I felt an unexpected pang of affection for Rachael. My Wikipedia search for the Muffin Man informed me that "Victorian households
had many of their fresh foods delivered; muffins would be delivered
door-to-door by a muffin man" and that the first mention in literature
of "The Muffinman" occurred in Jane Austen's *Persuasion*. I couldn't

17. Internet acronym: "Shaking My Damn Head." Rachael does a lot of head shaking.
18. Rachael, via Facebook.

help imagining the contrast between the material circumstances of Rachael's existence and those of Anne Elliot, the heroine of Austen's novel. I'm pretty sure Rachael hasn't had fresh foods delivered to her home, unless you count pizza delivery. But the idea of the old English nursery rhyme finding its way into Rachael's account of Carly Jax's afternoon pleased me. I pictured us all in the same room with tea and muffins: Carly, Anne Elliot, me, Rachael, the muffin man. Maybe baby Josslyn with her new kidney would be crawling around on the floor in a pink onesie.

I wondered what Jane Austen would make of *General Hospital*, whether it would strike her as a futuristic version of her own novels or merely smut. I like to think that if Jane Austen lived today, she wouldn't be all *Masterpiece Theatre* and NPR, that with her penchant for romance she'd find an analog for her own Anne Elliot and Frederick Wentworth ("Franne") in one of today's GH couples, Lulu and Dante ("Lante") or Samantha and Jason ("Jasam"). If you read Austen's letters, particularly the ones she sent to her sister Cassandra during her time at Bath, you discover a woman as avid an observer of and commenter on human foibles as Rachael or I could ever hope to be. From an 1801 letter: "I am proud to say that I have a very good eye at an adulteress, for tho' repeatedly assured that another in the same party was the *she*, I fixed upon the right one from the first . . . She is not so pretty as I expected . . . she was highly rouged, and looked rather quietly and contentedly silly than anything else."[19] I'd love to dish about adulteresses on GH with Rachael and Jane, who likely would find analogues for her Anne Elliot and Emma Woodhouse and Elizabeth Bennett in the likes of Robin Scorpio-Drake and Lulu Spencer and Carly Jax.

Of course, Jane Austen in her nineteenth-century grave is forever

19. *The Illustrated Letters of Jane Austen*, ed. Penelope Hughes-Hallett.

lost to me except as the author of some of my favorite novels. Rachael, though, abides in Illinois.

> i am going on a fast and i had to give up something i love for two weeks so i decided to give up fb since i'm so addicted to it lol so if yall need me call, text, email me or u can just tweet me....#loving god and nothing else matters![20]

She lists her phone number in her profile, and I've thought about calling to interview her.

But I won't. Why? Because RachaelmzRayonce' Davis occupies an intermediary zone Facebook has opened up between the categories of "friend" and "character." If I were to meet Rachael on the phone or in person, the chasm that separates us—race, class, age, education level, religious affiliation—would become immediately apparent, gumming up the machinery, the easy flow of communication we experience in our Facebook posts. Consider that I'm an upper-middle-class white woman writer in her forties with a PhD, happily atheist and childless. In the "About Me" section on her Facebook page, Rachael describes herself:

> my name is Rachael some people call me Rayonce' because i love Beyonce' and i'm always talking about her and dancing like her, but hey what can i say she's my idol. i am a cool unique person to get to know i have a good heart and if you know me then you know that i'm a good person. i love kids, someday i want to have 30 kids lol. well not 30 but close to it. right know i am focusing on trying to be an actress/writer but it seems like you have to be in the right place and time for that unless some big miracle happen but thats my dream though thats what i really wonna be in life... life is hard and its also short thats why you have to live everyday like its your last cause you

20. Rachael, via Facebook.

never know it maybe. thats why you have to thank god everyday for waking you up, because without god their would be no facebook, no world, no you and no me. so i thank you god...

Facebook has allowed us to filter out the demographic elements that, in other contexts, would make our friendship unlikely. In this way, Facebook reprises the demographic flattening evident on GH, which offers viewers storylines that feature beautiful, shapely, wealthy, heterosexual, white[21] characters almost exclusively. There are no Rachaels in Port Charles, though few things would please me more than to turn on my soap one day and see RachaelmzRayonce' Davis hiding in the well-tended privet hedge in front of the Jax home, stalking the blonde and always glamorous Carly with a kitchen knife.

Last week, while I was working on this essay, I wrote the sentence "Though 'General Hospital' is currently going strong and in no imminent danger of being canceled, I remain vigilant and a little nauseated when I watch these days." Just two days later, news broke that the network had canceled *All My Children* and *One Life to Live*, the two soaps that precede GH on ABC.[22] In corporate-speak that sucker-punched thousands of loyal fans, the network's press release explained, "ABC is evolving the face of daytime television with the launch of two new shows." Translation: two venerated soaps will be replaced with shows that "focus on food from every angle."[23] Replacing "Love in the Afternoon"[24] with "Food from Every Angle" marks a shift in American

---

21. There are currently four black characters on GH, but only one has a dramatic storyline and, significantly, a visible residence (i.e., she exists outside of the workplace). Even today, most black characters on soaps occupy "helper" roles (nurse, bodyguard, etc.).
22. I've always thought of AMC and OLTL as GH's warm-up acts.
23. The show that will bump AMC—with the inimitable Susan Lucci, who has played soap icon Erica Kane since the show's inception in 1970—is called *The Chew*.
24. This slogan, used from 1975 to 1985 to market ABC's daytime lineup, has become a shorthand among soap fans to refer to soaps' raison d'etre.

appetites, particularly those of women. The press release for *The Chew* begins, "As food has become the center of everyone's life . . ."

Really? What happened to love?

And when "food from every angle" blows Port Charles off the face of the earth, what will Rachael and I have to say to each other?

Wendy Rawlings

On "Why I Hope My Soap Opera Will Outlive Me and Other Confessions about a Dying Art"

Breaking the Fourth Wall

In Neil LaBute's movie *Nurse Betty*, Renée Zellweger stars as a waitress who suffers a nervous breakdown after seeing her husband murdered. She manifests her trauma by becoming obsessed with a character on *A Reason to Love*, the soap opera she watches. Zellweger's character, Betty Sizemore, can soon no longer distinguish between the character and the actor playing him. She's so traumatized that she drives cross-country and wangles her way onto the set of the soap opera, where the other actors believe she's auditioning for a role by staying in character. But for Betty, in the aftermath of witnessing her husband killed, reality and fantasy have collapsed into one undifferentiated experience. Not until the actors rehearse multiple takes of a scene does she come to realize that she's on the set of a TV show.

Seeing *Nurse Betty* made me realize how deeply invested I'd become in *General Hospital*, which I've been watching for more than thirty years, but also in an online community of viewers and actors on the show. This realization led me to reflect on the way that online communities have begun to erode the previously hard division between people we know in real life and characters in fiction. Similarly, online communities have complicated the definition of the word *friend*. Do you count among your *friends* people you converse with online every day but have never met in real life? Or do you reserve the honorific *friend* only for people you grew up with or see in person on a regular basis? What might it mean for fiction if our twenty-first-century definitions of *friend* have become more striated and multifarious?

I wanted to write a piece that both demonstrated and commented on how fully integrated into my life my online community of GH fans and actors has become. What started as just a TV show I love to watch has burgeoned into a virtual community in which viewers as well as the actors themselves comment on the genre many of us call "the never-ending story." As one critic remarks, "The soap is a relentless series of beginnings and middles, with no final solution." By its very definition, the soap opera goes on and on. Like life, it can be tedious and repetitive, with no sense of an end. And, as in life, none of us wants to think about the end.

I also wanted to enact a contradiction I have not been able to resolve. On the one hand, my interactions on Facebook and Twitter should reaffirm that *General Hospital* is entirely a fiction. After all, when an actress like Laura Wright makes a comment on her Twitter feed about the scene her character, Carly Jax, played that day, shouldn't I, like Nurse Betty, be startled into seeing the separation between actress and character? At the same time, though, the amount of conversation and commentary we (viewers and actors) devote to the goings-on in Port Charles serves to reify this fictional city and its inhabitants, turning it into a place I sometimes think about more than I do Tuscaloosa, the actual city I live in.

Online communities have made invented worlds (like those on TV) come to seem more real, whereas the real worlds we inhabit (often while sitting in front of our computers) become more abstract. I wanted to explore (rather than opine on) the ramifications this development might have for how we make and consume art. As one of my students last semester remarked, pointing to her laptop, "I live most of my life in here."

Ryan Van Meter

Monster

The first room was a graveyard. A wrought iron fence stood black and brittle in front of a sagging tomb, a few slanting graves and a knuckle-bone tree naked of its leaves. The ground beneath the tree wasn't real ground—neither grass nor worn-down dirt—but black and shiny garbage bags stretched out flat. Regardless, I believed it was a graveyard, never mind that I was in a school building, and knew I was walking over the square vinyl tiles of a classroom though it was too dark to see my white sneakers. The tiles were exactly like the ones lining the floor of my third-grade classroom across town. And never mind that I was walking with my dad, that he'd just bought us tickets, that he was right behind me as we followed a line of strangers who had also bought tickets to walk through this graveyard of trash bags instead of grass and black paper instead of sky. Never mind all of it when the plastic ground split and from its hole sprang a vampire. He stood taller than all of us and his white hands curled over the fence inches from my own white hand clinging to it, and his cape with its red lining like a tongue after cherry candy filled everything my eyes could see.

I jumped against the soft wall of my father because all of a sudden there was too much feeling to fit inside my skin. The vampire had been so well hidden that I hadn't even seen the possibility of him, and it was the fact that he had come out of nothing, that he could not be *there* and then be *there*, without ever arriving. Across our town in that classroom of mine was my desk, also waiting in the dark, and in the back of it, hidden, like the vampire had been, was my stash of plastic game pieces. One by one, I had stolen them from their respective board games. I rarely played games with my classmates when we were stuck inside during recess due to rain or snow. I usually sat at my desk drawing with markers from the big bucket in the back of the room. But when the bell rang, I leaned nearby my classmates and watched, waiting in plain sight for a piece to fall as they were cleaning up in the frantic minute before class resumed. I bent for the piece—the die, the tiny metal shoe, the carved wooden letter, the tiddlywink, the white marble—and tucked it into the palm of my hand and then dropped it into my pocket. And while Mrs. Grove sat in her rolling chair on the rug in the front of the room, I pulled the piece from my pocket and slowly, noiselessly slid it to the back of my desk behind my pencil box.

After the graveyard, a corner, a hallway with buzzing saw noises, a scientist making a beast in a laboratory with sparking blue currents, then another corner, a doorway, more darkness. My dad and I were suddenly alone with three white wooden doors—those old doors with the keyhole and the knob that jiggled as you turned it. Somehow it was utterly quiet in the room with the three doors. "Try one," my dad nudged, and I reached forward to the closest. It turned in my grip, but the door didn't budge. I stepped to the next and reached, but before my hand could get there, the door opened by itself about an inch, and the yellow face of a witch lined up one eye in the crack. I knew she was not a witch, that she was a regular person wearing a mask of craters and bumps. And that the gross hair pouring out of her hood was also not real, and that her hood and coat and everything else were what she wore and not who she was. Her hands didn't even match. They were normal hands, not yellow.

Under that mask could have been anyone, anyone at all. "It's not that door either," I said, barely.

And then he lifted a corner of the wall, also black garbage bag, thin and crinkling, and there was suddenly a small space like a mouth for us to pass through, and then we were in a hallway of a school again, with humming white lights hanging above us and a glass door at the end leading to night, and we were standing with our strangers, and everyone was taking deep breaths and laughing and putting one hand to their chest and pressing it there as though it was morning after the first bell and we were at our desks, facing the same direction because it was time to talk to the flag.

Halloween was a few nights later, and I trick-or-treated like every other kid. After dumping over my paper grocery sack on my shag carpet to sort candy into good versus boring, I dug through a bag of costume stuff in my closet. In the pile of rubber masks were the deflated slippery faces of a red devil, a green grinning beast (probably the Incredible Hulk—on whom, in TV show form, I had an intense crush, possibly my first, unless the Six Million Dollar Man was first), and a frowning clown, which was the best of them. Originally worn by my mother, who was a teacher and dressed up at school every year, this clown mask featured its own hair, red, curly but sparse, with enough white scalp to cover almost all of my own hair when I wore it. My mother had worn this for her costume as a regular clown—a clown who is funny—but what I recognized in its face on Halloween night was a certain amount of menace. It was sloppily painted in white, and black whiskers around the mouth and chin pushed through his makeup. Hastily smeared purple marks arced above and below the eyeholes, and a dark red nose sat in the center of his face, above his deep frown. I stretched it tight and snapped it over my head.

From my bedroom window, I watched the shapes of trick-or-treaters floating along the sidewalk. It rained every year on Halloween during the whole of childhood history, just as it did on Fourth of July, but not that year. A trio of creatures stepped off the next-door neighbor's porch, marched across the grass, and turned toward my house. A ghost wearing tennis shoes, a pirate with plastic knife and absent eye, and one of those kids who just wore the clothes he'd worn that day at school and carried his pillowcase as though that could properly be called a costume.

My own costume was already a mess across my twin bed. In jeans and a T-shirt, I ran down the hall to the door in our kitchen to our dark garage, and as I did, I pulled off the hook the wool plaid coat of my dad's that he wore when he raked leaves. It was so big, the hem hung past my knees. Outside, with socked feet on the cement, I wiggled into the chilly green-stained sneakers he wore when he mowed. As I slipped out between my bike and my mother's car, the boys stomped up our front porch and reached a finger to our glowing doorbell. My mother opened the door and they shouted their greeting. All three boys sounded older than me, at least by a grade, or maybe two. Maybe from my school, but maybe not. My mother stood with her large aluminum mixing bowl heaped with candy. She counted out the same number of pieces for each boy, and I thought I heard the candy drop into their pillowcases. They thanked her.

I didn't have a plan, there in my giant coat and clown face. I was a passenger to my feet in Dad's old shoes. I arrived at the mailbox, pinned into the grass at the curb near the corner of our driveway. Just before the boys on the porch turned with their candy, I leaned over its black hump, slung my arms and head over its other side, and then froze. The dark cement of the driveway was all I could see out of my eyeholes, and all I heard was the scuffling of sneakers getting closer, step by step by step, to the corner where they would turn to the sidewalk. The boys' voices whispered and laughed once, until their shoes skidded and the footsteps stopped, and I felt the attention of their eyes like heat.

"Hey, you guys," one of them said. "What is that?" And it didn't move, the clown, which was the thing about it, it didn't seem to notice they were there, it didn't seem to be there *for them*, it had just sort of fallen out of the clouds. Plus, the body. Big feet like a man's held skinny, slack legs into a big coat. And so it was hard to tell if the body filled the coat that didn't even look like a clown's because it wasn't purple or anything, and there was no plastic squirting flower. It didn't move, not one bit, so they walked again, but as they passed it, the white face lifted, and the eyeholes and dented red nose followed the eyes of the one who just came out with the pirate and ghost at the very last minute, whose gaze couldn't let go of the clown, until the boy whispered, "That is weird," into the backs of his friends, and his feet started to scramble across the grass.

And I knew that on any other night I would be the skinny, younger kid by myself as usual, just hanging over a mailbox like a total weirdo, the kid they would never pick for their kickball team, who, if found slumping this way, would be yelled names at, or maybe even have rocks kicked toward, but that night, because it was that night, I was a monster.

Preparations for the following Halloween began weeks in advance. From the scrap pile in the basement, I wrangled pieces of wood about the size and thickness of the thinner volumes of the encyclopedia standing in the glass bookcase, like maybe the I. To these pieces, I nailed narrower boards to form a cross. I painted them on an outspread *Post-Dispatch*, brushing gray and brown all over, drawing in details and dates and RIP with red and yellow and green. Packages of cottony fake spiderwebs were purchased with my allowance, as were plastic spiders by the sackful and a cellophane bag of rubber snakes, insects, bats, and a single fat rat, knotted together and wiggling. A cardboard skeleton with joints at the joints was posed and taped to the glass of the storm door. In the basement, in the dog's room, which he shared with the constantly humming deep freezer, I found a small wooden trunk with a hinged lid. Maybe four feet long and a foot wide as well as deep, this trunk was shiny deep crimson for some reason, which immediately reminded me of blood, so it was tipped over and emptied. Wads of newspaper were wrapped in a few yards of black polyester until they resembled a body-ish cylinder, and more paper was stuffed into a new mask whose face was a bald shrieking creature with wandering teeth and actual eyebrows of white springy hair. This creature rested in the blood coffin, which was laid aslant in the rock garden in front of our ranch-style house, and its lid was propped open, so it appeared that whatever supernatural force had wrested this coffin from the ground of our landscaped front yard had done so without disturbing the soil, to resurrect a creature in a child's tiny coffin with an old man's face.

And instead of trick-or-treating like other kids, I stayed home, screwed a red lightbulb into the front porch fixture and unwound an extension cord from inside the garage to plug in my record player, which I'd hefted from my bedroom. *Chilling, Thrilling Sounds of the Haunted House* by Disneyland Records cackled and whimpered from the shadow of an evergreen bush my dad trimmed once a year in spring. Pumpkins were carved assembly-line style: me scooping the slippery guts, my mother slicing the faces because she could draw ones that actually showed emotion—a howl, sneer, or gasp—and I just drew faces with bad teeth. Wearing a pair of my own jeans, I crammed myself into a pair of my dad's, buttoned up a red and blue flannel shirt, also of his, along with his army jacket from Vietnam, then shoved into a pair of his boots and a pair of his gloves and pushed my face into my clown mask. As darkness sank over our street, which was really a cul-de-sac, and the children of the neighborhood pulled costumes over their heads and painted their faces, I lay myself over the gravel of the rock garden, my shoulders against the sharp lip of the porch, my whole body held in the broken pose of a scarecrow, and waited.

One by one, dozen by dozen, in the damp dark of evening, trick-or-treaters walked down the sidewalk to our house, marched across the curving pavestones to our porch, and as they stomped up the slab where

I rested, where I looked like nothing more than a stuffed dummy—this yard is pretty cool, isn't it, with the red air and the spiders and that coffin, and that dead army guy is kind of scary—I sprang and reached for them with my gloves and growled, and they screamed and leapt—which was a thrill like joy because no one was ever afraid of me.

A few years later, we moved to a brand-new house in a subdivision where every house looked different from every other house, and where none of the streets had names. Bigger than our last one, we watched it being built piece by piece when we visited it every afternoon. First, it was craggy tan Missouri dirt, then there was suddenly an our-new-house-shaped basement as though space junk fell from the sky to land on our little acre. Then boards made the bones of the rooms and drywall hung from them, and then windows, and carpet and faucets, and then we moved in.

Our new porch was so much bigger, the new pavestone path so much longer, I needed to draw a map to plan for Halloween night. But this new house's best feature: two thick, square brick posts standing guard on either side of the sidewalk leading to the front door. They were like a castle's pillar sawed in half, with glass lamps perched on top. And reaching from each of these pillars was a very real and very sharp wrought iron fence, enclosing our shrubs, rocks, new red maple, and porch, and it was obviously a better, grander graveyard in waiting.

There were other boys in this subdivision, but they didn't go to my school, or if they did, they were so many years older, we may as well have gone to different schools. The kid next door was also named Ryan, and we were close in age, and we both had little brothers four years younger than us who were our enemies, and so we hung out sometimes, but usually only during summer. And there were two other boys the same age as my brother; the three of them had tried playing together but they didn't like the same things. These boys wanted to sit in one or the other's dark bedroom, blinds screwed tightly against the sun, and play video games or listen to music that their mothers were always telling them to turn down, where my brother wanted to drive tiny cars along the carpet and make engine noises with his mouth, even if he was a bit old to be doing so. By road, the house of the boy where the two boys spent most of their time in that dark bedroom was all the way over on the other side of the subdivision, across the pond. But from the front of my house, I could see the back of that one, and the flickering blue bedroom window. On the first Halloween night in that subdivision, the other Ryan and a friend he knew from Catholic school went trick-or-treating together in another subdivision because supposedly there were more houses, and these houses were closer together, so in less time you could come out with more candy. I didn't care about candy.

My mother had sewn an amazing costume. A monk's brown cloak, with a hood and actual sleeves and a separate belt for tying up the front. It was pretty long too, and my sneakers only barely showed beneath its careful hem. This costume was slipped over the head like a T-shirt and worn with a new mask—that of a skull with a melodramatic black crack down its forehead and beautifully ruined teeth. The terrible dark eye sockets revealed my eyes when the mask was on, which contradicted the entire concept of a skull but looked really, really cool. With hood up and mask on, I didn't look anything like myself.

When night arrived, and the moon rolled to its divot where it would sit in the sky, I stood next to one of the brick pillars. Of course, the lightbulbs in the lamps had been unscrewed and replaced, that year with murky blue. I held a fake battle-axe, the handle planted in the rocks next to the sidewalk, propping my body on its blade, my head bowed. I tried again to look like a dummy, a stuffed thing, a statue instead of a boy. The trick-or-treaters wound the path to our front door, turned to walk between the brick half-pillars, and as they passed, just as they wondered if that thing was real or not—the thing being me—I tipped my skull into the blue light and growled and raised my axe. They screamed, and it worked every time.

The next year, the year I was fourteen, I knew I needed to do something else. To scare them, I had to surprise them, and to surprise them, I had to be different. It didn't matter what costume I was in, if I was the lone figure in the walk to the porch. So I took safety pins and newspaper and a pair of my jeans and one of my long-sleeved flannel shirts and I made a stuffed version of myself, going as far as stuffing this dummy's ankle stumps into a pair of my boots I didn't wear anymore and fastening gloves to the ends of his sleeves. The pair of us sat in identical poses against the brick lampposts under the previous year's blue lightbulbs, because after being wrapped in newspaper and laid carefully in the maroon baby coffin, they still worked.

With my curtains of cobwebs, painted tombstones, rubber bats, and snakes, our front porch had gained quite a subdivision reputation. They all wanted to see what I would come up with — the families with small kids, the people who drove in from other subdivisions, the kids who were around my brother's age. When the trick-or-treaters came, they might have known one of the bowed figures on either side of the walk would jump and snarl at them, but they didn't know which, so when it was finally me who did, they screamed. Maybe even twice as hard.

The two boys the same age as my brother trick-or-treated that year in costumes that were barely costumes: the mask thrown over the face with the same clothes worn to school that day. By that point, they had a subdivision reputation too: for being obnoxious. My mother often pulled aside the blinds to complain about their long hair and unlaced boots and black clothes as they slogged across our lawn. Bowed in front of my lamppost, I recognized their shapes in the dark as they walked up the driveway. They would have been about twelve years old.

As they walked, too slowly for some reason, my eyes through my mask watched for the toes of their boots to touch the crack in the pavement that was my signal to jump. But right before they crossed it, they lunged at my twin, the stuffed dummy, and flung their arms at him. Tiny explosions lit up around his empty boots as sharp cracks split open the spell of my Disneyland record. Snap-N-Pops, those paper pouches of gunpowder that came in their own box of sawdust, sold at the fireworks stand only in July and presumably saved since. As the pouches broke all around the dummy of me, I sprang at the boys and growled as I wished I'd done the second before and forced a great laugh out of my mask at them. They'd tried beating me at my own Halloween game, but they'd picked the wrong me.

The innovation the following year, the final year of the front porch graveyard, was to stuff another dummy to make a trio of us waiting along the path to the porch. I also built a rickety kind of trellis that trick-or-treaters had to walk through. Two one-by-ones were stood up next to the lampposts with a third nailed across their tops, and then the whole thing was painted black, coated in fake webs and draped with rubber creatures—the same annual tangle of sticky bats and centipedes. After I strung it all up, I dragged my two dummies to their spots in the rock garden, leaving a blank space for myself, and went inside for supper.

And as they always did, the trick-or-treaters came, and they screamed when I jumped, and then they went to the door clutching their chests, and my mom opened it and gave them candy. I'd known that the two younger boys would come by too, probably in makeshift costumes like always, armed with their Snap-N-Pops. But I also knew that with three identical dummies, waiting and staring back eyelessly, their chances of guessing the right one were worse than the previous year. That they had each other, and I had to make my own companions from newspaper and old clothes, would not occur to me until later.

It also wouldn't occur to me until later, decades later, that my mother never asked me to consider that I was getting too old for Halloween.

That I was a teenager a couple of times over and still spending the night alone on cold gravel to thrill a bunch of strangers. When I finally fessed up to her that I was gay, also decades later, she would tell me a story of my childhood. One Saturday afternoon when I was around nine years old, the year I was stockpiling those game pieces in my school desk like candy to be savored later, I came in from outside and went straight to my bedroom. She peeked in her face as I put on a record, sat at my desk, and started pushing colored pencils across my wide, white sketchpad. Her boy in red shorts and red hair, prone to talking to himself in a range of voices, to skipping instead of running, was bent over a drawing of something—a lady in a dress beside a castle?—while the rest of the neighborhood children played outside in the street. From where she stood, she could see and hear them. She asked me why I'd come in.

"I don't know," I said.

"Well, did something happen out there? Was there a fight or something?"

"No," I shrugged, and then said without a note of sadness in my voice, "I'm just different from all the other kids," and kept drawing.

From my dark graveyard, I saw the two boys creep up the road. I had learned through years of practice that holding myself perfectly still, turning my gangly body into a statue, wasn't actually about holding. It was about letting go. If you tried for stiffness, to be a durable, immovable thing, you wiggled and gave yourself away. But if you let it all go, allowed your joints to loosen, you could fool people into thinking you weren't real, that you were a shirt full of newspaper instead of bone and blood. It was better with a mask on, where they couldn't see you watching them. Although wearing a mask for a long time isn't easy because you keep breathing in your own sweat and spit.

The boys' hands were stashed in their pillowcases, and as soon as they turned from the driveway to the pavestone path, they walked faster, with sudden purpose and urgency. Right past the first stuffed guy, without even glancing at him, and then past the second, as though he were invisible, not even there. They trooped right to me, pulled their hands back, raised their arms in unison, and slammed down on me a pair of water balloons. Through binoculars trained on our front porch, they had watched me unfurl my lump of spiderweb cotton, hang my bats, and set up my two dummies, so they knew which of the three was the real me, hiding in plain sight. He thinks he can hide behind a mask but he can't.

The balloons burst against the rocks, and I hopped the same way I did when the vampire burst from the ground. I wasn't very wet some-how, but it didn't matter. I was the scared one. And wondering why they'd tried so hard, two years in a row, to get me to jump and scream led straight to asking why I had wanted the same, year after year, for stranger after stranger. They liked feeling powerful, they liked feeling that they weren't powerless, like maybe they did every other day of the year from corner or sideline in their weirdo clothes. At least that's the common ground I imagined we had, though we were standing right then on opposite sides of it. When I heard their laughter, with their faces tipped back and split open, I hoped my mother wouldn't hear our commotion because I didn't want her to come out and see what had happened. "Very funny," I lied through my mask, which I couldn't take off. "You got me," I said, and waited with dread for the sound of the front door, opening.

Ryan Van Meter

On "Monster"

The Immersion Effect

The room empties of its light and all of us become quiet. In only seconds, there is no more weird room, no more strangers sitting in chairs in concentric circles, no more of my writing students that I've dragged here and made sit in the darkness with me. Dragged here without knowing exactly what is about to happen, though of course, I know what's *supposed* to happen, what my friend said would happen when he recommended it to me. "I want to take my students on a field trip," I told him. "Some immersive nonfiction experience." And he said he had just the place.

And now I'm sitting in darkness I haven't seen since that time in sixth grade when I went spelunking with the Science Club. (Long story.) We sit and the sounds begin. We've been promised soundscapes—effects, atmospheres of noise, music—and this performance of sound will do *something*. What, exactly, we'll find out in a few seconds. The old gentleman who escorted us into the theater, dear and sweet, if not a little kooky, had promised us waking dreams, or long-forgotten memories unlocked, or hallucinatory visions. All from sitting in the utter dark to listen.

But there was more design to all of it than that, of course. The sounds weren't random, they had been carefully chosen and patterned for their evocative quality, for the way they might sound *in the dark*. And the way we would hear them had also been designed—there were some two hundred speakers built into and around this weird round room. Hidden behind the geometric panels covering the walls and in the floor, but most of them hanging from wires tethered to the ceiling—so many hanging that they seemed to form another ceiling under the actual ceiling. All those wires—spindly, black, and glistening—remind me of the legs of crickets. And this room too had been designed, decades ago. With its white curves and diamond doorways and red carpet, it looks how someone might imagine a spaceship looked in 1960, so it feels simultaneously futuristic and outdated.

The music, when it begins, is soft and synthy, like the music playing in the corner of a yoga class, until it breaks out in quick reedy bursts, like a xylophone falling down a staircase. Slipping in and among the notes then are the evocative sounds—a baby laughing, cicadas humming, raindrops thumping on leaves, horses hammering across dirt, and even a train skimming down its track with all of its show-off noise. It's all a little hokey.

And I know I'm supposed to let go, to let happen whatever will. To let my mind *go* where it will. I think about the phrase "lose my mind," which suddenly seems morbid: if I lose it, will I be able to find it again? Like running around my apartment, checking all the places where I normally throw my keys, and not finding them, not on the dining table or in the bowl in the foyer or on the fireplace mantel or my nightstand, and then there, I spot them, on top of the refrigerator?

But what I've asked my students to do as they sit with me here in this utterly dark chamber of soundscapes is to let go, to lose their minds. I'm actually requiring they lose it for a grade, but it seemed a lot easier when I wrote the assignment sheet than it feels now in practice.

I said *immersive* to my friend, and that was accurate, but more specific might be that I wanted to create for my writing students an *aesthetic* experience. We read and studied Annie Dillard's "Total Eclipse" and David James Duncan's "Cherish This Ecstasy," both essays that describe the activity of the writer's mind during an intense aesthetic experience.

Both are writers who let go, who lost their mind, however temporarily, and then tracked its runaway charge and all of its show-off noise. So Annie Dillard had the spectacle of sun and moon aligning, and David James Duncan the extremes birds go through to survive and the transcendent inspiration that's created in him personally when he sees them, and we, we have the shushing of ocean waves moving above our heads as the sound in real life can never do. All of us writers will be aware of some external sensory event that creates (oh, I hope so) inside the mind an interior event of perception. And all of us will grapple (or will pretend to for a grade anyway) with what it means to experience something extrasensory—so overwhelming of our five senses that our minds are lost.

My essay "Monster" was inspired by the field trip that was supposed to inspire my students. (And it did—they turned in many wonderful essays.) As I sat there in the dark, once I stopped worrying about what I was supposed to be getting out of the experience and just started *experiencing*, I realized that the soundscape unfolding all around us was just loud enough to mask the actual ambient sound in the room. Sitting on all sides of me were strangers in chairs just like mine, but I couldn't hear or see them, and cut off from them in that way, I began to feel alone. I *knew* I wasn't alone—I knew that I'd come with fifteen people. I was probably the most un-alone a person could be, actually. But I felt alone. And I started thinking about being alone.

Behind my family's second house, the "new" house in my essay, and across a wide, dry field, tucked in the curve of trees on the far side of a clearing was a wrecked house. It must have been left mostly empty before it was bulldozed, and then its ruins just lay there, for months. On silent Saturday afternoons, or sometimes after school, before my parents returned home, I walked to this old gone house. I liked that the pile of broken junk was still somewhat house-shaped. The splintered beams covered in the pink guts of insulation, electric cords hanging out of tubes, torn, limp sheets of vinyl tile. Broken glass, bent nails. So many dangers available in one small spot. And I didn't do anything while visiting this house besides sorting through its trash for treasure, of which there was none, because of course I'd already checked, and still I returned. Other people, maybe even kids my age, would have been scared of such a place, but not me. And I liked it because they weren't there.

And then some sound or another—footsteps, perhaps, or the hammering of the horses—reminded me of my Disneyland haunted house record, something I hadn't thought of in years. How those evocative sounds were patterned into soundscapes to scare. To drop a listener suddenly into a dungeon, a forest or a wing-beat belfry. Even when it wasn't Halloween, I used to sit on my shag carpet and listen to this record over and over as though those sounds were my favorite songs and I was singing along.

Then, I realized, even if the sounds playing in the spaceship room were of rain or laughing children, I was laid across a rock garden wearing a clown mask and hoping to scare some neighbors by jumping at them. It didn't matter what my senses were registering, I was paying most of my attention to the interior event of my consciousness. And somehow, my mind had gone from the solace and comfort of loneliness to Halloween, and my childhood obsession with dressing up. What did being alone offer me? What did being masked offer? I wanted to understand that connection better—if there was a connection there at all—and "Monster" is the result of that inquiry.

That kind of activity of the mind—trying to think through how we get from one seemingly unrelated memory to another—is a strategy that gets a lot of attention in my essay-writing classroom. It can be applied to any subject, any memory, any inquiry. But because I was sitting in the dark as I came to the curious connection between Halloween and loneliness, while feeling utterly detached and alone among strangers, I wanted to emphasize in the essay the concealing quality of masks. Several times and from several perspectives, I imagine my way into the perceiving eye of another person, and I look at and describe myself as they might have seen me. Masks seem to have some kind of power. Without any certainty about the real face underneath it, we seem to fear the idea that the mask could be hiding *anyone*. Our skinny, lonely neighbor or a lunatic, we're not sure.

In that technique, quiet as it might be in the actual essay, I saw my piece as being able to do what a mask also does: try on different ways of looking and being looked at, take on different identities. I got to be my mother, the ne'er-do-well subdivision kids, and various trick-or-treaters. This is the most explicit exploration of nonfiction's boundaries, though it might also be said that any representation of the truth is always only that: a representation. I was aware while writing "Monster" that I was pushing hard on the credibility of nonfiction and that my reveries into the consciousnesses of other people risked the believability of my whole piece. But the technique wasn't random, of course. It was thematically linked to the essay's subjects. In fact, it was *borne* of the inquiry of the essay's subjects. I thought of it precisely because I felt so comfortable in this strange, lonely place I had written myself into. And if we can't push against convention in the pursuit of our hardest questions, when can we ever? If not when we're making truth into art, then when? And if we don't take advantage of such opportunities, if we turn away from innovation out of an anxiety about "the truth," isn't that reluctance simply another kind of dishonesty?

Writing Exercises

Marcia Aldrich's "The Structure of Trouble"

Make a list of ten words (the number is arbitrary — it could be fourteen or twenty) that play a defining role in your life. Go through the list and pick the one that compels you the most, even if you don't understand entirely why. In fact, it would be better if there is some mystery as to why this word draws you. (All the better to write about.) I chose a common word, a frequently used word, not a word used for its novelty, like *defenestration* (to throw something or someone out of a window). And it's a word whose meaning changes depending on who is using it and in what context. Yet, generally speaking, we understand its import.

This writing prompt might work best if you choose an equally common word whose abstract meaning is easily grasped but whose personal significance is yet to be discovered. Some other examples might be: *pain, satisfaction, belief, silence, trust, melancholy*. Begin writing about what your associations are with the word, what stories or questions are attached to this word, what problems. Research the word — does it have a history? How do other people use the word? Begin to think about creating your own narrative with the word using a "found" structure such as the diagram, the outline, the companion, the inventory. The point of using a found structure, though you are invited to innovate upon that form, is twofold. You are emptying that form of its accustomed contents and filling it with something unfamiliar, thus creating a kind of friction between the familiar and the unfamiliar. So, too, such a disciplined form provides tension and contrast, perhaps resistance, to the overwhelmingly personal material.

Monica Berlin's "The Eighteenth Week"

What happens when we take a firsthand account and give it breathing room? Does this new distance allow us to separate ourselves from the experience? And can a personal essay reach greater depths by taking away the personal?

As demonstrated in "The Eighteenth Week," try working through a real-life event in the third person. Pick an event that means a great deal to you, but rather than retell it as you have before, replace the lyric I with the fictive *he* or *she*. How do a narrator's capabilities change when a first-person story is told in the third person?

If you're up to it, experiment further by writing near-identical essays from different points of view. Which version best recounts your story?

Eula Biss's "Time and Distance Overcome"

While journalism and the personal essay share many borders, one major difference is journalism's attempt at neutrality. In a personal essay, the writer can take sides all she wants, though this "taking of sides" would likely be frowned upon if printed on the front page of newspapers.

Attempt to create your own personal essay–journalism hybrid by taking an important date in your life (or in the life of a parent or grandparent) and doing some research to see what other occurrences took place simultaneously. A good place to start is the microfiche collection at your local library. What was the front-page headline on the day you were born, on your parents' wedding day, on the day of a grandparent's death? Essentially, we're asking ourselves: What connections can be drawn between one's personal life and the world at large? Allow serendipity to get to work and find out.

Ryan Boudinot's "An Essay and a Story about Mötley Crüe"

How often have you started a sentence, "It would be so cool if . . ."

Now what follows the "if"?

In this exercise, indulge your wildest fantasy. If Mötley Crüe's not your band of choice, then curse somebody else's tour bus to break down in front of your parents' house. Or better still, move beyond celebrity sightings and make yourself the hero. How cool would it have been if you had actually made the game-winning shot rather than thunked it off the backboard?

You get the idea. Give yourself a chance to live out the dream you never lived yourself. Test yourself under these conditions, because you never know, just maybe—under the strangest of circumstances—those dreams may one day come true.

Ashley Butler's "Dazzle"

While the "dazzle" technique was originally used for military purposes (a form of camouflage), experiment with how you might apply similar techniques to your written work.

How might you write an essay that is simultaneously visible but not? That is, while the reader sees one layer of your work, how might you create a secondary layer beneath the surface one that is felt but not directly viewed?

Or try thinking of it another way: How might you write a piece that encourages a reader to *feel* something beyond the words themselves? Hemingway called this technique the "Iceberg Theory," of which he noted, "If a writer of prose knows enough of what he is writing about he may omit things that he knows and the reader, if the writer is writing truly enough, will have a feeling of those things as strongly as though the writer had stated them."

Experiment with this theory, placing pressure on particular moments throughout your work to evoke emotions not initially felt on the surface.

Steven Church's "Thirty Minutes to the End"

Choose a meaningful event you did not witness firsthand, though one that involves people you know. After interviewing these people, attempt to retell/reimagine their story. Feel free to employ drama, suspense, and all the techniques of realistic narrative.

For an added challenge, try to keep the first-person I on the periphery, working it in only occasionally to suggest your role as investigator and explorer rather than main character.

Stuart Dybek's "Bait"

Memory has its limitations. How we recall an event is often greatly at odds with how another might recall that same event. This difference in interpretation could be the result of an array of factors: mood, vantage point, and selective memory, among others. Yet how might a writer exploit these different versions of truth within the essay form?

Begin by honing in on a childhood experience shared among family. What do you remember most vividly? What remains fuzzy? Begin by simply recounting the event, being sure to include every sensory detail available to you. Next, test your version against those of your family members by asking them to share their versions. What details were lost on you but resonated with others? What contradictions within the narrative begin to emerge?

As you write your essay, make allowances for the shortcomings of memory by offering multiple interpretations and perspectives of the same event, thereby prompting the reader to parse the fact from the fiction.

Beth Ann Fennelly's "Salvos into the World of Hummers"

Write about something in nature using the form of the thing to shape your essay. How would an essay about a weeping willow, for example, be different from an essay about a honeybee or an emu or a cancerous cell? Consider how they exist in the world: what characteristics are most well-known, most secret? How can the thing itself inform the writing?

Robin Hemley's "Flagpole Wedding, Coshocton, Ohio, 1946"

We've all seen a movie poster claiming its subject to be "based on a true story." The question, of course, is, "What do they mean by 'based'?" When we watch a film that boasts such a claim, we're often left wondering precisely what details were added to better hold our attention (as well as what truths were omitted to keep from boring us). Similarly, the phrase "based on a historical account" is equally problematic—leaving the watcher/reader to question where history ends and fiction begins.

Try writing a short story that is only "based" in fact. Decide what factual liberties will be taken and why. What effect does this new freedom offer you? Similarly, if you were to transform your "based on a true story" story into a nonfiction essay, how might you make it clear that not every word is confirmed? Consider how genre informs myth, memory, and rumor as you attempt to tell your tale.

Naomi Kimbell's "Whistling in the Dark"

How can controlling the tone of a piece alter its overall meaning? For this exercise, think back to a humorous interaction that occurred over the past few years and attempt to tell it in a solemn manner. Then, reverse it: take a solemn situation and try to make it humorous (a far more difficult task). While we expect mental illness to be an issue of such importance that it can only be represented in a serious manner, what is gained by viewing it in a different way?

Keep the story but alter the tone; then ask yourself, "How have I changed the story?"

Kim Dana Kupperman's "71 Fragments for a Chronology of Possibility"

Write your own set of fragments.

First, select a title of another work (a poem, film, song, book, short story, etc.) to define the number of fragments you will write (i.e., "Thirteen Ways of Looking at a Blackbird," "When I'm 64," "Land of 1,000 Dances," "19th Nervous Breakdown," "Eight Miles High," 8½, *Six Feet Under*, *Seven Brides for Seven Brothers*, 10, etc.).

Second, alter the title slightly but retain the number.

Third, choose a poem or piece of prose that you have read and love; use a line or sentence from it as a prompt to write the fragments. Some examples:

"And another regrettable thing about death . . ." (John Updike, "Perfection Wasted").

"No one perhaps has ever felt passionately towards a lead pencil" (Virginia Woolf, "Street Haunting").

"Let the light of late afternoon . . ." (Jane Kenyon, "Let Evening Come").

"We started dying before the snow, and like the snow, we continued to fall" (Louise Erdrich, *Tracks*).

Paul Maliszewski's "Headaches"

Describe something that's difficult to convey. Pick something ineffable and give it a concrete, comprehensible reality through your description. Try different methods of description, as demonstrated in "Headaches." Don't rely solely on physical detail. Employ metaphor, for instance, both simple, jarring metaphors as well as more complicated models. Experiment with narrative techniques, too. For a longer project, keep a journal devoted to some subject of interest to you, regularly recording your impressions. The journal should be focused on a particular subject and not, say, a diary of everything you did over some period of time.

You should be selective about what you put into the journal. Think of yourself as the editor of your experiences. After some period of time — a month, a semester, whatever the assignment allows — use the journal as the basis for an essay. Don't copy one to the other. Instead, see how much of the journal you can leave out, cutting down what seemed worth noting at the time until all that remains is crucial and evocative.

Michael Martone's "Asymmetry"

Try writing an essay in which you make good use of the page. That is, don't settle for the conventional 8.5 x 11-inch, portrait view. Instead, consider writing your piece on a different spectrum altogether. You might consider landscape view, various dimensions, or colored sheets of paper.

Or, consider writing your essay on a medium other than paper — a canvas, a receipt, tree bark. Of course, not every subject lends itself to these experiments, but when you settle on a subject that opens itself up to unique opportunities, be sure to experiment with this space.

Ander Monson's "Outline toward a Theory of the Mine versus the Mind and the Harvard Outline"

Consider the essay as "a space to be filled," and remember: you are the one doing the filling. How might you fill the emptiness of a page? What tack will you take?

While words are, perhaps, the most obvious way to fill space, what other possibilities are at your disposal? Graphics? Diagrams? Charts? Photographs? Maps? Equations? Grave rubbings? Ticket stubs? Squashed insects?

As you begin your essay, consider how words might be weighted equally alongside some other tool at your disposal. Allow words to provide one stream for your narrative, but experiment with other streams as well.

And think about visual appeal. What does your piece look like on the page? How does this visual representation speak to the themes you're addressing?

Dinty W. Moore's "Four Essential Tips for Telling the Truth in Personal Memoir and Securing That Blockbuster Book Deal"

Nobody's father ever returned home to brag about the bluegill ("a little on the small side") caught on his most recent fishing trip. Instead, Dad's bluegill is often transformed into a great Northern pike or an oversized alligator gar, and there wasn't just one of him, but ten, maybe even a hundred! In fact, now that he thinks about it, those monster fish had him surrounded, and if it wasn't for Dad's quick thinking and fishing prowess, it was only a matter of time before . . .

Long story short, we call them "fish tales" for a reason—because no one believes for an instant that Dad is telling the truth.

But how might writers exploit this breed of exaggeration for comedic effect while remaining truthful to the experience? How can we write first about the pike or the gar before knocking the fish back down to size?

Begin by recounting a story in its wildest incantation, and as your essay moves forward, try replacing the exaggerations with truth. How might we skillfully replace the pike with the bluegill?

Allow humor to play a role. Don't be afraid to call out our writerly instinct to conflate our own fish tales.

Susan Neville's "A Visit to the Doctor"

How might one report the personal in an impersonal manner? Obviously, the omission of the I (or to put it another way: changing the point of view) is one technique, but what other techniques might be available to you? What other ways might you create distance between you and your story?

Also, consider how altering the tone in this way changes the reader's experience. Does the reader place more faith in a story told in a more objective manner, and if so, what is lost as a result?

In this exercise, recount a personal event in your life through someone else's vantage point. You need not necessarily omit the I, but simply recount a story from another figure present in the scene. What might he have observed from his vantage point?

Brian Oliu's "Contra"

Think about your favorite game as a child: this can be a video game, a sport, a game that you made up with siblings or friends. Attempt to explain how this game works to someone who is entirely unfamiliar with the game—pay attention to the small nuances, the absurdities of the situation, the world that one must embrace to be a part of this experience. While describing the game, start to inject small personal anecdotes about the game and the people you played it with—who they were, where they are now. Imagine yourself playing this game now: what changes would you make, would it be easier/more difficult?

Lia Purpura's "Squirrel"

Very often we have to set up the conditions for surprise and freedom. You can begin to do that by lowering the bar. Really lowering it. Sounds contrary to the general, ambitious American goal of "aiming high," doesn't it? What I mean is, try to consider your work a "sketch" for as long as possible. Ideally, this will shake you out of your fear of writing "badly" and allow for a deeper, more patient form of exploration. When we set our expectations too high, we often find ourselves demanding premature completion or mastery. To demand too much too early is not unlike asking a newborn to do a backflip—totally inappropriate to the being's developmental stage.

How to set up the conditions for surprise practically? As you're working through a piece, try to vary your entry points: go back to your journal and start troublesome sections anew. Write by hand if you usually type. Read your work in very different settings (in a park, in a coffee shop . . . anywhere other than where you usually work; you'll hear differently and be caught up by fresh angles previously unseen). Vary the place in the piece where you enter (start work in the middle, at the end). "Keeping it new" requires work!

Wendy Rawlings's "Why I Hope My Soap Opera Will Out-live Me and Other Confessions about a Dying Art"

Whether you acknowledge it or not, likely you're the world expert on something. And even if you're not "the" world expert on, say, shoehorns of the nineteenth century, if you know *anything* about shoehorns of the nineteenth century, you're probably somewhere in the top three.

It's time to put your bizarro knowledge to good use. Rather than shying aware from your peculiar obsessions, embrace them. After all, someone has to write about shoehorns, so why not you? Allow your passion to drive your work (even if that passion is somewhat embar-rassing, or at least not the first fact you bring up at the dinner party).

Begin by brainstorming a list of five "obsessions." Then dig deeper, trying to figure out what, precisely, you love about these things. After settling on your obsession, write about it in a manner in which it has never been written about before—you can focus on form, organiza-tion, style, or simply depth of knowledge. (And it helps, I might add, if your interest happens to be uniquely yours.)

So embrace your eccentricities, make them yours.

Then share them with the world.

Ryan Van Meter's "Monster"

Take yourself to an immersive, aesthetic experience. An art exhibition, a performance—especially of some art form you don't normally seek out. A local curiosity, like a giant camera obscura perched on the ocean, or a museum devoted to the history of the grain elevator, or a cyclorama of taxidermy birds. Hike to some unusual terrain. Watch the sun set on the summer solstice, the year's longest day. Spelunk. Almost anything will do, and all you have to do while you're there is experience.

A day or two later, think over the perceptive experience you had. What happened inside your brain—the activity of the mind—as you were immersed, aesthetically? You're not trying to write a review of the experience, and you might not even mention it; instead you're trying to create a kind of record of your mind's blips and beeps. Once you scribble down all the places your mind went as it was lost, interrogate them. Is there a strange connection that you'd like to learn more about? What is your individual and particular process of perception? What happens to *you*? And how does investigating that process complicate your sense of yourself? Or what does it reveal?

It's entirely possible nothing essay-worthy will come from your notes. That doesn't mean you're a bad perceiver or that your mind lacks activity. Try again another time. Regardless, you went somewhere interesting and saw something new.

Contributors

Marcia Aldrich teaches creative writing at Michigan State University. She is the author of *Girl Rearing*, published by W. W. Norton and part of the Barnes and Noble Discover New Writers series. She has had essays appear in *The Best American Essays*, *The Beacon Book of Essays by Contemporary American Women*, and a wide range of literary magazines, such as the *North American Review*, the *Seneca Review*, and the *Gettysburg Review*. She has been the editor of *Fourth Genre: Explorations in Nonfiction*. In 2010 she was the recipient of the Distinguished Professor of the Year award for the state of Michigan. Her book *Companion to an Untold Story* was selected by Susan Orlean for the 2011 AWP Award in Nonfiction and was published by the University of Georgia Press in 2012.

Monica Berlin's recent work has appeared or is forthcoming in *Hayden's Ferry Review*, *Ninth Letter*, *Witness*, *Diagram*, *Rhino*, the *Southeast Review*, *Third Coast*, the *Missouri Review*, *Fourteen Hills*, *New Orleans Review*, and *Memoir (and)*, among others. "The Eighteenth Week" was published in *Passages North*, where she was awarded the 2009 Thomas R. Hruska Memorial Prize in nonfiction. She is the nonfiction editor for *Fifth Wednesday Journal* and the project director for "The Knox Writers' House," a digital archive of contemporary literature. Currently an associate professor at Knox College in Galesburg, Illinois, Berlin teaches creative nonfiction, poetry, and fiction, focuses on late twentieth- and twenty-first-century American literature, and serves as the associate director for the program in creative writing.

Eula Biss is the author of *The Balloonists* and *Notes from No Man's Land*, recipient of the National Book Critics Circle Award. She holds an MFA from the University of Iowa and teaches nonfiction writing at Northwestern University. Her essays have recently appeared in *Gulf Coast*, *Harper's*, *The Best Creative Nonfiction*, and *The Best American Nonrequired Reading*.

Ryan Boudinot is the author of the novels *Blueprints of the Afterlife* and *Misconception*, a PEN/USA Literary Award finalist, and the story collection *The Littlest Hitler*, a *Publishers Weekly* Book of the Year. He teaches at Goddard College.

Ashley Butler is the author of *Dear Sound of Footstep*. She has a BA from Columbia University and an MFA from the University of Iowa. Her work has appeared in the *Believer*, *Ninth Letter*, *jubilat*, *Gulf Coast*, *Creative Nonfiction*, and *pool*. She lives in Texas.

Steven Church is the author of the books *The Guinness Book of Me: A Memoir of Record*, *Theoretical Killings: Essays and Accidents*, and *The Day After the Day After: My Atomic Angst*. His work has been published in *AGNI*, *Fourth Genre*, *Brevity*, *Colorado Review*, *Wag's Revue*, the *North American Review*, and many other journals. His essay "Auscultation" from the *Pedestrian* was selected by Edwidge Danticat for inclusion in the 2011 *Best American Essays*. He's a founding editor of the literary magazine the *Normal School* and teaches in the MFA program at Fresno State and for the University of New Orleans low-residency MFA program.

Stuart Dybek's most recent books are *I Sailed with Magellan*, a novel in stories, and *Streets in Their Own Ink*, poems. His fiction, nonfiction, and poetry appear regularly in magazines, and his work has received numerous awards. Dybek is distinguished writer-in-residence at Northwestern University.

Beth Ann Fennelly directs the MFA program at Ole Miss and lives in Oxford, Mississippi, with her husband and three children. She has won grants from the NEA, the Mississippi Arts Commission, and United States Artists. Her work has three times been included in *The Best American Poetry* series. Fennelly has published three full-length poetry books. Her first, *Open House*, won the 2001 Kenyon Review Prize and the Great Lakes College Association New Writers Award and was a Book Sense Top Ten Poetry Pick. It was reissued by W. W. Norton in 2009. Her second book, *Tender Hooks*, and her third, *Unmentionables*, were published by W. W. Norton in 2004 and 2008. She has also published a book of nonfiction, *Great with Child*, in 2006, with Norton. As a contributing editor to the *Oxford American*, she frequently writes essays on southern food, music, and books.

Robin Hemley is the author of ten books of fiction and nonfiction and the winner of a number of awards, including a Guggenheim Fellowship, two Pushcart Prizes, and many others. He directs the nonfiction writing program at the University of Iowa and is also the founder of the NonfictioNow Conference. His work has been published in the *Believer*, *Creative Nonfiction*, *Orion*, the *New York Times*, *New York Magazine*, the *Wall Street Journal*, the *Southern Review*, the *Sun*, and many other publications.

B.J. Hollars is the author of *Thirteen Loops: Race, Violence, and the Last Lynching in America*, *Opening the Doors: The Desegregation of the University of Alabama and the Fight for Civil Rights in Tuscaloosa*, and *Sightings: Stories*. He is also the editor of two additional anthologies: *Monsters: A Collection of Literary Sightings* and *You Must Be This Tall to Ride: Contemporary Writers Take You Inside the Story*. He is an assistant professor of creative writing at the University of Wisconsin–Eau Claire.

Naomi Kimbell is from Missoula, Montana, where she lives and writes creative nonfiction. In 2008 she earned her MFA in creative writing from the University of Montana. Her work has appeared in *Calyx*, *Black Warrior Review*, *Indiana Review*, and the *Iowa Review*. "Whistling in the Dark" is listed as a notable essay in the 2010 edition of *The Best American Essays*. She lives with her husband of eight years, a dog, and a bird at the base of a mountain that looks like an elephant in repose.

Kim Dana Kupperman is the author of the essay collection *I Just Lately Started Buying Wings. Missives from the Other Side of Silence* (Graywolf Press, 2010), which received the Katherine Nason Bakeless Prize in nonfiction. Her work has appeared in many literary magazines and anthologies, including *The Best American Essays 2006*, *Brevity*, *Fourth Genre*, *Ninth Letter*, and *River Teeth*. The founder of Welcome Table Press, a nonprofit independent press dedicated to publishing and celebrating the essay, Kupperman is the visiting writer-in-residence in nonfiction at Fordham University and a faculty member of Fairfield University's low-residency M FA program. She also coordinates the *Gettysburg Review*'s Summer Conference for Writers.

Paul Maliszewski is the author of *Prayer and Parable* (Fence Books, 2011) and *Fakers* (The New Press, 2009).

Michael Martone was born in Fort Wayne, Indiana, and went to the public school there, attending North Side High School during the years they took to renovate the old building. The construction went on all four years of Martone's time in high school and the students worked around the workers who closed first one wing of rooms then the next, sending classes looking for a new space or reclaiming a room now rewired or freshly painted or floored with new terrazzo. The electricity for the master clock in the principal's office had been cut early, and all the clocks in the hallways and classrooms found their own separate times. Most stopped. Some sped up, swept ceaselessly, or stuttered in place as if it was now impossible to move to the next second or the next, sticking with each tick, mesmerizing Martone with a cruel montage of what was now becoming his lost and wasted youth. The period bells, the commencement and dismissal bells, had quit ringing months ago, and the space of time when the students changed classes was marked in gritty silence. A rudimentary PA system had been jerry-rigged, tinny speakers and exposed wires, and each morning the guidance counselor squeaked that the official North Side time was whatever it was. Everyone set his or her watch, regulated for the rest of the day, shuffling through the debris and drop cloths in the work light–lit hallways. It was here Martone first studied chemistry in the fifty-year-old laboratories on the third-floor east wing that would be the last to see repair. He still has his slide rule, army surplus, in its leather case. The hairline cursor embedded in the sliding glass indicator, he realized, was a real hair. He learned to manipulate the contraption in the oversubscribed extra credit slide rule seminar after the regulation lab session. There, too, in the chemistry labs, he saw, for the first time, his teacher perform the Old Nassau clock reaction. He mixed the solutions in the big Pyrex beaker to first produce a pumpkin-orange precipitate as a mercury compound settled out and then, after several seconds, the bright orange suddenly turned to a liquid lamp-black as the excess iodine left over transmuted to starch and turned on its color, a black curtain dropping instantly. The demonstration was meant to astound with its alchemy, and Martone was astounded, asking to see again the chemical logic of it, how benign soluble concoctions created a product that became a new reactant that then was ready to react. He liked both the anticipation and the rapidity of the transformations, the visual demonstration of whole moles being stewed in their own molecular juices, the quick switch and then its double-cross. It was called a "clock" because of the predictable ticking of the bonding and unbonding that timed out perfectly, a collection of ionic seconds spinning on their own internal clocks. This led to this and that to this. The equal sign is replaced by arrows in a chemical reaction, one thing after the other. Years later, when he was a senior in organic chemistry, Martone asked the teacher if he could, in his spare time, work on constructing a new clock reaction that would, this time, express itself in North Side High School's colors, red and white, not out of any school spirit but mainly out of an urge to tinker with the watch-works of cooked-up nuclei and electron shells. After all, the class he was taking spent its time knitting together long compounded chains of carbons and hydrogens and oxygens, matrices of esters and ethers, another kind of ticking, the proteins twisted into the worsted zipper of a gene undergoing mitosis, another two-step through time. In that lab, too, he set a girl's hair on fire with the Bunsen burner, the flame eating up the long straight strands of her long brown hair like a fuse, another illustration of time. The burned hair, turning to ash, flaked, crumbs of a rubber eraser, spilling to the floor as the stink of it, the hair burning, rose in almost visible solid cartoon waves of wavy stench, the glow of the actual burning peeling now in the nape of her neck, the instant chemical reaction of it, giving off its own unique rainbow of bright colors. They had been performing primitive, spectral analysis, igniting unknown compounds held in little wire loops over the lip of flame, reading the combustion's signature through the slit of a cheap prism tube. The tip of her hair sparked as Martone tipped the burner toward what turned out to be a sulfuric something or other. Martone damped down the crawling flicker with his hand, his fingers flouncing the hairs that wove themselves into a now-ratted cap, a nest, and for a moment it seemed that the whole canopy would ignite, enriched by the addition of fresh air. Martone was left holding this halo of fire, a hat from hell, a melodrama of oxidation, when, just then, the teacher pulled them both in to the emergency shower where they were doused and, just as suddenly, engulfed in wet smoke and sodden hairy ash. Martone never did find the combination of compounds to create the clock reaction in his school colors. He remembers poring through old manuals his teacher gave him with pages of tables listing reactants and products and their shades of colors, valences and radicals, ions and elements, metals and base. He wandered through the old laboratory's closets looking for odd specimens in ancient glass bottles stopped up with moldy cork or decaying rubber stoppers, the forgotten chemicals undergoing their own unsupervised and unrecorded experiments, reactions oxidizing into clumps of rusty rust, bleached stains, inert crystalline sweating salts, the paper labels foxing, the beakers mired in viscous goo, and the wood racks gnawed at by some now long gone acidic lick. Helping to clean out the closets in anticipation of the renovation, Martone garnered extra credit to offset the disappointment and possible average grade for his disappointing independent study. In the mess he found the apparatus used through the years to create the famous Old Nassau clock reactions for succeeding classes—the tinctures of iodine, the compounds of starch, the granules of potassium, and the etched graduated cylinders set to deliver the proper quantities of chemical ingredients for the demonstration of time all that time ago. Years later, Martone is on the phone to his classmate from those years whose hair he set on fire during an experiment meant to identify certain chemicals by the spectrum of light they emit when set on fire. Martone has taken to looking through his past lives, has found many of his former classmates by employing the emerging electronic technologies online. He lives now far away from Fort Wayne, in Alabama, and finds it difficult to return home for the sporadic reunions, and when he does, others from back then now live even farther away or seem to have disappeared altogether. He thinks of it as a reconstitution, as hydration, this telephoning, and admits that his efforts redoubled after the collapse of the towers in 2001. That collapse seemed to be a kind of boundary, a membrane, a demarcation as narrow and fine as the hair fused in glass on his slide rule, of before and after. He found her, the woman whose hair he set on fire in his high school chemistry lab, living in New York teaching organic chemistry, of all things, at Columbia University there. The irony was not lost on them. She explained to him that she now was attempting to isolate low-molecular-weight chromium-binding substance in human urine. It had something to do with diabetes and insulin and iron in the blood. It was late at night and they had been talking on the phone for a while about the past and chemistry and what they had both been doing separately at the same time during all those years when suddenly Martone heard band music. It was past midnight. The music, even diminished by the telephone, was distinctively brassy and rhythmic, shrill and thumping. Martone identified it as "The Horse," a favorite of their own high school's pep band years before. "Oh that," she said. "It's Columbia's marching band. A tradition. They spontaneously appear on the night before the orgo final and march around the Upper West Side." No one will believe this, Martone thought. After all these years, no one will believe such coincidences of time and space. He learned long ago in the sciences classes of his high school that there were these things called constants. Gravity was one. The speed of light, he remembered. And time—time was constant too.

Ander Monson is the author of a host of paraphernalia, including a decoder wheel, several chapbooks and limited edition letterpress collaborations, the website http://www.otherelectricities.com, and five books, most recently *The Available World* (poetry, Sarabande Books, 2010) and *Vanishing Point: Not a Memoir* (nonfiction, Graywolf Press, 2010). He lives and teaches in Tucson, Arizona, where he edits the magazine DIAGRAM (thediagram.com) and the New Michigan Press.

Dinty W. Moore is author of *Crafting the Personal Essay: A Guide for Writing and Publishing Creative Nonfiction* as well as the memoir *Between Panic and Desire*, winner of the Grub Street Nonfiction Book Prize in 2009.

He worked briefly as a police reporter, a documentary filmmaker, a modern dancer, a zookeeper, and a Greenwich Village waiter before deciding he was lousy at all of those jobs and really wanted to write memoir and short stories. Moore has published essays and stories in the *Southern Review*, the *Georgia Review*, *Harper's*, the *New York Times Sunday Magazine*, *Philadelphia Inquirer Magazine*, the *Gettysburg Review*, *Utne Reader*, and *Crazyhorse*, among numerous other venues. He is a professor of nonfiction writing at Ohio University.

Susan Neville is the author of eight collections of fiction and nonfiction. She is a winner of the Flannery O'Connor Award and the Richard Sullivan Prize, and her stories have appeared in two Pushcart Prize anthologies. She teaches at Butler University in Indianapolis and in the Warren Wilson MFA program for writers.

Brian Oliu is originally from New Jersey and currently lives in Tuscaloosa, Alabama. His work has been published in *Hotel Amerika*, *New Ohio Review*, *Ninth Letter*, *Sonora Review*, and elsewhere. His collection of Tuscaloosa Missed Connections, *So You Know It's Me*, was released by Tiny Hardcore Press in June 2011. His collection of lyric essays based off of video game boss battles, *Level End*, was released in April 2012 by Origami Zoo Press.

Lia Purpura is the author of seven collections of essays, poems, and translations, most recently *Rough Likeness* (essays, Sarabande Books, January 2012). Her awards include a 2012 Guggenheim Foundation Fellowship, finalist for the National Book Critics Circle Award (for the essay collection *On Looking*), NEA and Fulbright Fellowships, four Pushcart Prizes, work in *The Best American Essays 2011*, the AWP Award in Nonfiction, and the Beatrice Hawley Award in poetry. Recent work appears in *AGNI*, *Field*, the *Georgia Review*, *Orion*, the *New Republic*, the

New Yorker, the Paris Review, and elsewhere. She is writer-in-residence at Loyola University, Baltimore, Maryland, and teaches in the Rainier Writing Workshop MFA program.

Wendy Rawlings is the author of two books, *The Agnostics* and *Come Back Irish*. Her work has appeared in *AGNI*, *Atlantic Monthly*, *Indiana Review*, *Tin House*, and other magazines. She is a faculty member in the MFA program in creative writing at the University of Alabama and loves all dogs.

Ryan Van Meter's essay collection *If You Knew Then What I Know Now* was published in 2011. His work has also been published in journals and magazines and selected for anthologies, including *The Best American Essays*. He lives in California and teaches creative writing at the University of San Francisco.